I0707999

A Manner of Expression

A MANNER OF
EXPRESSION

Why Contemporary Black Expressions Offend White People

A Manner of Expression

A Manner of Expression:
Why Contemporary Black Expressions
Offend White People

Copyright 2023 - Brian C. McGuire
Library of Congress 1-12185269351

All rights reserved. No part of this book may be reproduced unless
agreed to by the author.

ISBN: 13: 979-8386642631
IMPRINT: Far-Left Publications

Printed in the United States of America
10 9 8 7 6 5 4 3 2 1

Without limiting the rights under the copyright reserved above, no
part of this publication may be reproduced, stored in or introduced
into a retrieval system, or transmitted, in any form, or by any means
(electronic, mechanical, photocopying, or otherwise), without the
prior written permission of the copyright owner.

The scanning, uploading, and distribution of this book via the Internet
or via any other means without the permission of the author is illegal
and punishable by law. Your support for the author's rights is very
much appreciated.

A Manner of Expression:
Why Contemporary Black Expressions Offend White People

by
Brian C. McGuire
Towson University

FAR LEFT PUBLICATIONS

Brian C. McGuire

A Manner of Expression

Brian C. McGuire was born in Baltimore, Maryland on May 31, 1970. He spent thirteen years serving in the United States Armed Forces. He received a Bachelor of Science from Towson University. His areas of research interests include the mental terrain of Community Psychology: A field of Human Services that places special emphasis on problems associated with urban groups and how they adapt under low socioeconomic conditions during childhood, adolescence, and throughout the course of adult development and aging, and sociocultural influences (including theoretical concepts pertaining to how various dimensions of culture influence stress and coping). Brian is also the author of several exceptional indie reference books to include: The Color of Our Souls: How Multi-generational Experiences Impact Our Lives, Refusing to Learn: Really, How Dumb Do You Think I Am? and Against Black People: The European Will to Conquer.

TABLE OF CONTENTS

Dedication

It does nothing for us to hoard knowledge. If we cannot share it, then we teach the world nothing. Teach them so they may learn. If they refuse to learn, then guilt them into learning. The time is now!

Acknowledgements

This book was written at my home in response to a historical argument about White people and their discomfort, uneasiness, and inherent fear of Blacks. Amid a multitude of discussions on race, culture, and ethnicity, it became apparent that the time was right to give the world insight into the lives of Black people. Who they are, where they come from, and what they're all about are questions most of us will never know until we submit ourselves to discussion. So, after a few advisory discussions on the topic, the idea for this book began to take form.

These advisors participated in discussion topics for the primary and final draft of the manuscript. I would like to thank them for their hospitality, advice, and encouragement in their efforts to help me write this book:

I owe a profound debt of gratitude Yvonne M. Drake. She is a wonderful source of support who always assistant me in my writing projects. Her commitment to my quality of writing is most appreciated. She is invaluable to me.

I would like to thank Kyndra Rhodes who has given special insight into various aspects of this book. Her role as a special consultant helped me communicate clearly the intricacies of this book. I thank Kendra for her time, contributions, and the support she has given me in the writing process of this book.

Finally, I'd like to express my continued gratitude to Anita L. Opher for her expertise on my writing projects. I gratefully acknowledge her ongoing assistance on this project.

I thank each one of them for their continued support. They are greatly appreciated.

Prologue
On a Manner of Expression

Like his other reference books, Brian C. McGuire's approach to reference book writing is, at best, controversial. Throughout this book, you will read how the meaningful and unique ways Black people express themselves elicits some of the most thought-provoking concerns for White people. Most Black authors restrict themselves to writing about topics concerning their own race. In this way, they choose not to break an understood truce foraged with their oppressors. Others have only begun to include bits and pieces of race-based literature into their work. A Manner of Expression: Why Contemporary Black Expressions Offend White People goes far beyond other reference books by discussing racism with an integrated socio-cultural lens throughout its content.

For far too long, reference books have been the domain of a single culture (Western) and a single identity group (White), a single sex (male), and a single social class (middle). Nonwhite identity groups and other identity groups, categorized as minority, have examined reference books only to discover deliberate attempts to coverup unpleasant facts that incriminate or charge Whites for crimes against humanity. The result is nonwhites, both student and professional, here and abroad, have been unable to find discussions about the many problems they confront in their daily lives. And, to worsen matters, most authors who write on topics that highlight problems of racial inequality, racial inequity, and social injustice have had their books removed from the shelves of mainstream book stores. If you were to conduct a content analysis on any books having nonwhite topics in mainstream book stores, you will find little, if any, entries.

Race, along with ethnicity, culture, and other identities, provides an important lens for understanding intergroup behavior. McGuire's approach provides a critical perspective for examining and curtailing social problems that prevent us from understanding who we are and how we should behave toward one another in a humane society. While most authors believe reference books are long overdue for a sociocultural overhaul, they do work as an etch-a-sketch to assist in the development of writing on more inclusive topics. Thus, classic reference books should be referenced, but only when appropriate.

Understanding McGuire, no reference book is ever wasted. Although some do not withstand the test of time, many failed attempts are recycled through the literature as an analysis in his quest for truth. Why? Such discrepancies or misinformation will often lead him and, sometimes, the reader in positive directions.

This reference book, A Manner of Expression: Why Contemporary Black Expressions Offend White People is a work of lasting artistic merit. Written with modest intentions, its purpose is to highlight the historical concerns White people have against Blacks and the creative ways Blacks express themselves. In it, McGuire documents how the overwhelming stress of oppression impacts Black people. However, the scope of discussion is narrowed to keep topics relevant.

A recurring theme in this book is how Black people show remarkable resilience, responsiveness, and adaptation in the presence of overwhelming stress and oppression. The hope is for the reader to form the impression that Blacks will eventually succeed despite having been exploited, oppressed, and humiliated throughout their intellectual history. Moreover, this book was written to ease into consciousness a reminder that as sentient beings, Blacks are naturally entitled to human rights as a fundamental principle of humanity.

We are all a part of the human condition not because people gradually developed into more complex beings, but because every lifeform is able to experience sensation. It is our sensations that create commonality. And commonality of interest ensures cooperation, which is the basis of civilization.

Societies are civil toward one another. But not every society is civilized. In a civilized society, people from every walk of life are able to experience wanted emotions like happiness, joy, and gratitude, and unwanted emotions such as pain, grief, desperation, and despair. It is a condition of our humanity that makes it so. America is a highly modernized society in today's terms. But, to deprive a people of their human rights, regardless of race, ethnicity, culture, sex, gender, age, language, ability, location, belief or religion, or national status, is cruel. So, to make Black people experience pain and suffering simply because of their skin-color is uncivilized, thus inhumane. Why?

Blacks are able to experience sensations or feelings, emotions, and response to impressions.

For too long, White people failed to comply with or simply have not respected the human rights of Blacks. Chattel slavery, two periods of eugenics, racial segregation throughout the antebellum South, lasting long after the Civil War, and prejudice and discrimination well into the new millennium shows a growing, long-lasting disrespect for the rule of natural law.

This book does not highlight White people's refusal to abide by natural law. No, that's not its intended purpose. However, it does give a moderate, unassuming description of the maltreatment endured by Blacks for which White people are assumed to be unfriendly or threatening. Since most topics discussed in this book are uncomfortable for Whites, critics will find it to be a provocative and questionable read. Why? It violates an understood truce to criticize White people for their willingness or continued efforts to break natural law.

Author Brian C. McGuire spent more than three decades struggling to make the topic of racism more assessable to the public. He also works hard to curtail the tendency to label as deficient Black people from which dominant White society mistakenly regards their beliefs and practices as ill-gotten, ill-conceived, or just wrong. He further believes that the psychology of Black people should not be teased apart from the fundamental beliefs and practices of mainstream culture but rather, examined, in concert, as a whole.

Introduction
A Manner of Expression

If you can't beat them, then guilt them into submission.

Brian C. McGuire in press

Hey, what can you say! White people are right. Blacks in America are inherently violent. It's true! The manner in which they express themselves demonstrate a willingness, near eagerness, to embrace violence, opened violence at that! Some people say violence comes from an ignorant mind trying to express itself. But, here is the question. Why?

Whites and other racial groups are also inherently violent. For example, my country, America, which is led and controlled by White people, has engaged in nearly every war on the planet since its early conception. In fact, America has not seen more than ten years of piece since its conception. If that's not enough to stimulate your thought processes, America is locked into war with approximately one hundred countries at any given time. So, why are Black people considered to be the most violent?

Some people say it's their nature. That Blacks are troubled over their inability to adapt to a vastly changing world. But, here's the problem with that line of reasoning. We see the same level of violence in any group of people who are in power as well as those who are oppressed to the end point of subjugation. I wonder which position Blacks are in today?

It is only common sense that an oppressed group of people resist domination when the oppressor acts cruelly toward them and for no apparent reason than skin-color.

The point here is if you subjugate a people to the point of oppression, their behavior will deviate from the standard norm and manifest itself in other, more deviant ways. Violence is one manner of expression.

Understand that oppression causes deviant behavior in most people. It is also true of Whites. The more you oppress a group of people, the more they will resist you. For any oppressor, all forms of resistance are considered hostile or acts of aggression.

There is a problem in Northern Africa where Black Africans are being trafficked across the Mediterranean Sea into Europe. Most are trafficked for the purpose of organ harvesting. We know this to be true due to the amount of news coverage America received on the matter. Yet, there is nothing to be done about it. And why not? Why do you think human trafficking exists on so many levels, even here in the United States of America?

The United States would like to traffic Black people through the legitimacy of the prison industrial complex. The idea is to rent out cheap prison labor for fortune five hundred companies to profit. Independent, privately owned companies are already contracted to build prisons and have done so for the purpose of openly exploiting Blacks on the free market. That and the fact that Blacks are considered a commodity on the New York Stock Exchange. To top it off, melanin is also a prime commodity of the New York Stock Exchange.

They're using melanin (pigment) as computer chips in computer-based systems. Why? It has the ability to transduce electrical energy. Can you imagine that? If that's not enough to anger you to the point of concern, we also have evidence of police corruption specifically against innocent Black people.

In many of the documented cases, police were recorded violating the civil rights of Black citizens. Evidence includes but is not limited to planting drugs and paraphernalia on the person of unsuspecting Blacks with the criminal intention of falsely incarcerating them. Most of those cases are documented hate-crimes. Yet, even with the nature of criminal intent, nothing has been done about it. Now, how does that tickle your fancy? If you're not under distress about the aforementioned, then it more likely does not apply to you. That or you exist on the opposite end of the racial continuum.

Black people are angry at the notion of having no control over their lives as they should. Many live at the minimum level of subsistence of which no human should have to exist. They are stressed out from poverty and other situational factors. They are also forced to endure chronic living conditions such as inadequate housing, dangerous neighborhoods, burdensome responsibilities, and economic uncertainties to name a few potent stressors in their daily lives. And while certainly other identity groups endure poverty, Blacks have been left marginal by the very people who oppressed them.

Marginalization refers to a process in which the oppressed loses cultural and psychological contact with both their traditional society and the larger, more dominant society. How does that happen? Dominant society exercises its power to socially exclude Blacks and to segregate them to neglected areas of American society. In many cases, Blacks develop feelings of alienation and identity loss. And what's the results? Well, Blacks dissociate from the cultural mainstream. And, they become disorganized and unsupportive of acculturating people. Given a few generations of existing as marginal or segregated, neglected, and impoverished, they will give the appearance of being inherently violent, shiftless, and lazy. Yet, under similar conditions, so do Whites.

Blacks know all too well how poverty imposes considerable stress on them and their families. The chronic living conditions they are forced to endure speaks for itself. Fortunately, Blacks develop important resources to offset the overwhelming stress of poverty. But often, that's taken from them in the form of government shutdowns (That's just what Republicans do). With a scarcity of resources and no economic system to balance the effect of poverty, communities wither, leaving them to become marginal. Marginalization leads to the notion of violence, crime, and other criminal mischief.

Still, there are other outlets to enjoy, outlets that enable Blacks to endure the daily hassles of chronic living conditions. Singing, dancing, playing games and participating in sports, reading, story-telling, even cooking are recreational activities that can be done by almost anyone under any given condition. War never stops soldiers from eating a meal. Crime never stops children from playing on the opened streets. And poverty never stops poor people from experiencing hope. Why not? It's the will of humanity. And, humanity is destined to succeed. Or is it?

What a curious progression for White people. Today, Whites are moving beyond the limits set by humanity. I once thought that the human condition was mutually exclusive with humanity. But White people have taken a dark and menacing path to achieving enlightenment. The human condition apparently dictates the will of humanity. It has something to do with God's divine plan or the right to free will in a manner of speaking.

While humans have the right to choose their own destiny (hence, free will), humanity governs their will but only as a source of influence, guidance, or direction. As humans evolve, humanity slips away, lacking the ability to govern human nature. What lies ahead is a brave new space in a world in which humans can continue to evolve. So, what happens when we move beyond the will of humanity? That's something else to think about, indeed.

As humans evolve into more complex beings, so too do their manner of expressions. Their attitude and behavior, their expressions of empathy, sympathy, and apathy, as a matter of fact, the entire way they exist changes. We'd like to think humans will evolve into meaningful and eloquent beings. But, fact of the matter is, it is their right to progress or digress, even to regress as I believe regression is not a part of the human condition nor the human will. Even if they attempt to explore freedom beyond the will of humanity, humans will endure.

One of the main problems with people today is the disconnection between humanity and the human will. Both are connected to nature. But since humans have the right to exercise free will, they will eventually move beyond humanity as part of the human condition. As they turn toward the stars in further search of conquest, the possibility exists that they will no longer be bound by their terrestrial states. Since human nature is a part of evolution, and evolution is an inevitable part of change, we need to understand it better and prepare for what will apparently happen next.

What We Can Do About It

What we can do to ease racial tension is recapture the characteristic spirit of culture. To accomplish this feat, you must first recapture that moment in time when people were defined by common interests. We deprive ourselves the feeling of kinship with others that results from sharing attitudes, interests, and goals in common. It's not always about finding new frameworks and languages but, most times, rekindling that which was lost, moments in time that defined who we were as a whole while rousing new hopes and aspirations that tell us where we are headed. Sometimes we must return to the point of conception in order to better understand how we got lost in the first place.

The second feat is critical as we must reconstruct our lives with new codes of conduct not considered necessary at the time of conception. This means to reassess the quality of our lives as it once progressed, together, in common interests. I'm not sure if ever there was a time in American history when Whites and Blacks ever progressed together. So, I am referring to a time when Blacks united together in solidarity and that unity aligned in common interest with like-minded Whites.

The notion of dissociating ourselves from various aspects of society tells the world that we are concerned chiefly with our own priorities. Such narrowminded views often follow selfishness and greed. Our failed economic system is more or less the result of such prejudiced views. Thus, our understanding of people and their lack of consideration is critical for us to rebuild our lives in common with those who share our characteristic spirit.

You can always tell who in society shares our characteristic spirit in common by their cultural upbring-ing. Each of us practice beliefs that reflect unique traditions specific to us. These traditions and widely accepted ways of behaving tell the world who share common interests. When we see children dancing to music on the open streets, we know it's an old-school style, behavioral characteristic of Hip-Hop culture. So, it is more likely they are the Black children of America. That or they are heavily influenced by the characteristic spirit of Black American culture.

Characteristic spirit of culture is a term that reflects the types of behavior, institutions, and norms found in various societies. It also speaks to the types of motivations and ambitions associated with a wide range of knowledge, beliefs, arts, laws, customs, potentialities, and habits of people who share commonality: what we call group-oriented behavior or ethnicity. So, now that you know: Did you also know you can tell what type of people you are dealing with simply by the types of institutions found in their societies?

Institutions, which are the results of long-standing and well-established customs and practices, simply tell us which priorities a society considers important. This understanding is profoundly necessary in order to rebuild a failing society. For example, America is a society that recognizes free speech as an institution of education. Therefore, it defines educational institutions as the hallmark of Western civilization. Institutions provide us a historical basis from which we can also define people.

A necessary skillset, we also need to single out social problems to redefine ourselves and better understand why people experience discomfort, uneasiness, and fear of change to the point of social separation. The types of institutions we build tells the world how complex a society we are beyond natural spoken language. It also tells the world whether we are a true civilization with an established democracy.

The last feat is a major challenge as it involves teaching our children to actually embrace the characteristic spirit of culture. Our children are growing up in a nihilistic society under the false impression that all religious and moral principles are worthless. Many of them consider life to be meaningless. I would say we have to reinvigorate them. But, since this generation of children have never known the meaning of love, sacrifice, and commitment, then how would they know to respond characteristically to culture? Most of them do not have the spiritual aptitude to build a new hope in a failing society.

So, how do we motivate a generation who's never known the benefits of freedom, the luxuries of liberty, or the pursuit of happiness even though it's an individual act to follow? This means we have to find people with a unique vision to motivate us all. In that way, we can form lasting connections to families. These connections will give new energy or strength to generations of people. The revitalization of energy or strength will make them feel healthier, and more alive, some, for the very first time. Then and only then can we make people more excited and interested in embracing the characteristic spirit of culture.

In order for these steps to work, everyone must hold themselves accountable. As we make our way through the new millennium, our challenge is to democracy and the fight against the tyranny of racial oppression. We live in a world filled with nihilism and a society full of xenophobic conflict in fear of White genetic annihilation.

In this introduction, we briefly discussed the psychology of White people and the problems they have with Blacks and their manner of expression. In chapter 1, we will briefly revisit their psychology of concern as reasons for why contemporary Black expressions offend White people. Then in chapter 2, we will have an in-depth discussion on the way Black people express themselves, hopefully, revealing a cascade of fascinating events that summarize their thoughts, emotions, and actions. These events often take place over decades, leading well into the new millennium, an era that I sometimes refer to as the age of new hope.

Earlier in the introduction, I gave a summary of reasons why freedom of expression potentially causes conflict between Whites and Blacks. Throughout the rest of the book, we will explore many aspects of contemporary Black expressions, from the way Black people behave in the public domain to the specific expressions they adapt under the system of oppression. The way they walk, talk, and the manner of cultural expressions that sets them apart from others will be discussed soon. But first, let's gain a better understanding of why contemporary Black express-ions offend White people.

Chapter 1
Why Contemporary Black Expressions Offend White People

A Manner of Expression

> If you can convince the lowest White man he's better than the best colored man, he won't notice you're picking his pocket. Hell, give him somebody to look down on, and he'll empty his pockets for you.
>
> Lyndon B. Johnson (1908 – 1973)

Former President Lyndon B. Johnson (LBJ) gave Republicans a blue print on how to continue racial division in America. Forty-four years later Donald J. Trump accomplished that feat. By recognizing and prioritizing the poorest White people in the country while ignoring the simple wishes of the most acculturated Blacks, Donald Trump won the forty-fifth US Presidency on behalf of the Republican Party. The country has been racially divided, existing in turmoil ever since.

Just think about the Republican attitude toward Democrats, Liberals, and Blacks, or about any nonwhite or any person categorized as minority. Now think about the reasons why dominant society finds Black people so offensive. Now, let's consider Black people and their attitudes toward Whites for a moment. Is it positive, negative, or somewhat liberal toward them? Or, is it independent of how they are treated as a people?

Some people believe that Blacks are more forgiving and accepting of Whites than Whites are of them. As we look at why contemporary Black expressions offend White people, two major concerns arise: Are Black people naturally aggressive? Or, are Whites displacing their aggression onto Blacks?

A Contemporary Approach

I guess I will have earned my keep if I can explain why contemporary Black expressions offend White people. Quite simply, contemporary Black expressions stand out above and beyond what Whites consider to be contemporary White expressions. Whites claim they express themselves in an unobtrusive manner. But what we know is they have done everything to oppress Blacks in order to stand out in social dominance.

White people enslaved Blacks, experimented on them, lynched Blacks in fear of social competition, even consumed their body parts for better protection against diseases. Still, Blacks rise to the occasion. That, in and of itself, is the reason why contemporary Black expressions offend White people. The odds they overcome is phenomenal in a manner of speaking.

The way Blacks walk, talk, dress, and behave is a manifestation of their triumphs over their trials and tribulations. That's the reason why so many White people are offended by the mere presence of Blacks. But that's enough appraising Blacks for now. Let's get into the thick of it!

For some odd reason, White people will not consider Blacks as a wholesome part of America's value system. Would it be a far stretch to consider if I say Black people are naturally aggressive? Or, would it be fair to say that Black people are naturally offensive to White people? That, quite frankly, Black people look scary? Their manner of talking, walking, and their outward appearance is followed by the belief that they are dangerous and likely to cause White people harm. In many cases, White people experience discomfort, uneasiness, and fear in the presence of Blacks. Are those statements true too?

The typical response is to say it's all of the above. We know of such matters because we experience them. Right? Everyone knows at least one person who is Black. Heck, most of us do not live in a social vacuum. We see related events on television too. We hear about it on various radio stations, et cetera. The media is constantly bombarding us with news about the crimes they commit. Besides, we know at least one person who experienced problems with Blacks. For the most, we experience such events through social interaction. So, it is what it is! It always appears to be the case with Black people.

The aforementioned appears to be the case for many Blacks today, even a few Whites. But, what if I told you that contemporary Black expressions are the result of racial oppression. And, the country is being overexposed to contemporary Black expressions through the use of mass media. Moreover, it is being integrated into your consciousness by way of indoctrination through the educational system. How would that set with you?

Black people are overly represented as criminals in mass media and network movie cinema. More often, they are depicted as inherently violent, shiftless, and lazy. Even today, although Black characters are being represented in positive rolls in iconic movies like Marvel Comics' The Avengers, a fictional movie geared toward heroism and bravery that gives credit to the potentiality of Black people, the average person is still overexposed to progressively more anxiety-provoking depictions of Black people on television and network film.

Movies such as Birth of a Nation (1915) depicted Black Americans as violent, shiftless, morally degenerate, and dangerous. It was one of many movie films used in the early nineteenth century to rewrite history through the use of White supremacy propaganda. The meaning of the movie conveyed an important message; and the message was and still is abundantly clear. There is nothing more to understanding Black people than their level of potential aggression. When it comes down to educating or informing Black people, why bother. What you see is what you get!

American history books tell a similar tale. Many accountings of Whites in American history depict them as Wholesome and morally upright people who selflessly sacrificed their own humanity to civilize Black people and the world left behind. In every turn of event, history depicts White people as having a disinterested and selfless concern for the wellness of others. World War I, the Korean War, World War II, and the Vietnam War, were selfless yet necessary actions taken to continue living under the blanket of freedom provided by the greatest nation on earth. When in fact, the opposite is true.

American history is a falsification of past events, especially in human affairs such as war and universal forms of interaction. History teaches us that White people failed in their attempts to civilize a people who are culturally and morally bound by ignorance. Black people are governed by their own prejudices and superstitions. Until the arrival of White people, many Blacks were nomadic and showed violence toward one another. Heck, they still do!

Such a depiction is the mindset many Whites have about Blacks today. So, when we learn that the government turns a blind-eye to states that enforce segregation, we believe it to be a necessary action to keep an undeveloped people from causing harm or committing injury to themselves and others.

We know many White people believe Blacks are undeveloped as a race. That when they fully evolve, they will learn to behave accordingly. That it is a question of evolution thus their inability that prevents them from succeeding. So many people believe Black people cannot survive in today's society. They say that their struggles signify a people who are desperately trying to stay relevant in a world that left them behind. Whites also say it is for this very reason, Blacks act out in violence.

So, the million-dollar question is why do contemporary Black expressions offend White people? They believe that it is the sheer absurdity of Black immorality, and all of the tragicomic elements associated with it, that causes White people to fear contemporary Black expressions. But that argument appears to be a good one, does it not?

Black people express themselves in a variety of ways. Usually, contemporary Black expressions are characterized by a special vividness. So, for generations, Whites believed Black people were seeking attention or White peer approval. It is said that Blacks would blow small problems out of proportion. That many of the problems Black people sought were overinflated just to elicit attention, sympathy, or pity from White people. In this way, Blacks become the focus of intense consideration.

Today, many Whites believe Black people seek out attention just to make their racial group the focus of White people's attention and admiration. Equality, racial equity, which is not to be mistaken for reparations, reparations, and violent crime are said to be attention seeking methods used to elicit a response from Whites. Whites claim that such unhealthy methods are symbolic of a greater problem; hence, Blacks are the White man's burden.

President Joe Biden also suggests Black people seek out positive validation through more sophisticated identity groups that are in tune with the values and practices of mainstream culture. Why? More Whites continue to believe that the manner in which Black people express themselves can and will result in the permanent loss of their sense of agency.

As a people, no other racial group on earth suffers the level of indignity Black Americans experience. Many groups claim tragedy that should not be ignored or forgotten. There was the Jewish holocaust, World War II Japanese American internment camps, the scheduled caste system in India, and many more places around the world where people suffered great tragedy and indignity. Yet, Blacks continue to endure at a loss of human dignity and sacrifice. They endure without the world's compassion for their misery or suffering.

Although advocates continue to demonstrate the importance of Black people, not only in American society but throughout the world, critics are adamant about teasing them apart from the daily lifestyles of mainstream culture. Segregation is the hallmark of conservatism. In this way, it has been a major thorn in the side of American democracy. Conservatism has also been problematic when rigorously fighting to improve the quality of living for Black people.

People who fear change are transfixed on America staying stagnant. It's not change in and of itself they fear. It's just abrupt change that brings them anxiety or so they say.

More than any desire, the ability to endure, achieve, or succeed, even under the most adverse conditions, is human nature. Thus, the notion of Black people resisting or fighting against the tyranny of racial oppression is disconcerting to their oppressors.

If you just missed it, this is what offends White people. Whites fail to understand the curious progression of Blacks. That is to say, they are at a loss as to why or how a people can endure such indignities when they have long since been the target of victimization. Blacks are the most vulnerable racial identity group on earth. Still, Whites take every opportunity to oppress them. Yet, Blacks continue to overcome with grace and dignity. They contribute to some of the most important aspects of American culture. And, for the most part, they do it in a meaningful and dignified way. And whites find their dignity to be offensive.

Raising the Argument

The problem of race, crime, and politics have been raised in arguing concern for the way Blacks express themselves, especially in public domains. Most of the concerns are geared toward the younger generation of Black American men with increased interest in young Black American women showing more irate behavior than Black men in recent years.

For example, in the early to middle 1970's, New York citizens like Afrika Bambaataa rid their communities and cities of gang violence and associated lifestyles through the use of more constructive outlets such as street dancing and rhyming songs. With the emergence of Hip-Hop culture, street gangs lost its place on the East coast, quickly becoming a West coast phenomenon.

Cliques began replacing the lifestyles of gangs on the East coast. *Cliques* are tight-nit groups who tend to bond quickly due to common interests or other shared characteristics. These groups love spending time together, stay true to each other until the very end, and will not allow outsiders to join their circle: often referred to as old-school cliques.

Then in the late 1980's through the 1990's, as drug violence began appearing on streets across America, street gangs began making its way back to the street of East coast cities. Young Black males were being charged with drug related criminal offenses with an increasing number of Black women appearing in court as drug dealers and members of notorious street gangs. Back then, in the 1990's, most of the violent crimes were drug related criminal offenses said to be committed by drug gangs, a term coined by the mass media. The crime data was more often collected using young Black men, and then general-ized to Black women who were arrested as drug carriers and users.

Night-after-night, media outlets appeared to vilify drug dealing while glorifying the lifestyle. The media depicts drug dealers as cold and calculated killers who will poison women and children with drugs just to earn a dollar. At the same time, they extol the benefits of selling drugs. The media glorifies them by discussing their lavish life-styles. Women, money, expensive cars, and fancy traveling experiences are among the rewarding benefits of drug dealing. As well, media personalities made no distinctions between drug gangs on the East coast and the violence brought on by West coast street gangs.

Critics continue to press for distinction between the two types of criminal activities. They hoped that network news syndicates would try to defuse the situation of drug violence by making distinctions between West coast gangs and East coast cliques. But their efforts were to no avail.

Mass media personalities would give increased attention to their term drug gangs, saying there was no difference between the criminal intentions of drug gangs and street gangs. They continued to prejudice their understanding of the two groups as gangs and biased their assumptions of both. Today, and for a while, the East coast has been flooded with gangs and gang warfare.

The Truth Behind Contemporary Black Expressions

Everyone would truly understand why contemporary Black expressions offend White people if it were only a matter of negative gestures or threatening behaviors presented. But, that's not the case. Blacks have tried to be productive citizens since their very first day of freedom (June 19, 1865). Unfortunately, the more productive Blacks become, the more socially resistant Whites become toward Black people. They create White supremacy groups and organizations that negatively impact every aspect of the Black experience. In fact, Whites are matter of fact about it. White people took part in countless massacres just to uphold White supremacy. Most of these massacres were designed to suppress voting rights, labor rights, LGBTQIA rights of Black and other nonwhite people, land ownership, economic advancement, education, and freedom of press as well as religion in the United States of America. Although racial violence impacts nearly every racial and ethnic identity group in America, it has been particularly traumatizing to Black Americans.

Massacres in the United States include but are not limited to The New York City Draft Massacre (the 1863 race riots), which is the largest civil insurrection in US history, second only two the Civil War (1865), the Fort Pillow Massacre of 1864 where five hundred union soldiers, the majority Black American, lay dead or massacred after they surrendered to the Confederate Army, and the Ebenezer Creek Massacre where Blacks who escaped from slavery were cut off from crossing Ebenezer Creek, which led to their death.

It's balls to the wall for White people! Certainly, Whites are the most violent people the world has ever seen. They kill with maximum effort or commitment to maintaining White supremacy. Blacks, Whites, Hispanics, anyone advocating for the fundamental rights of nonwhites, will be killed just to maintain White supremacy. Although the list of massacres is in no way complete, it does sketch out the level of violence Whites are willing to inflict on a people simply to maintain White supremacy.

The murder of Black people, state sponsored or otherwise, has always been to maintain a sense of superiority over them. One would seem to think that if Black people would only stop pursuing the same ambitions or any type of ambitious activities, and just keep their heads down and work, White people would leave them alone. But, to the contrary, that is untrue.

White people will not rest until Black people are extinct. Black people never agreed to be colonized. But, they tried to be better citizens. They adopted Christianity and tried to learn the habits of Whites. Blacks acquired the knowledge of White people: their history, laws, beliefs, and politics. Still, Whites refused to accept Blacks on the basis of skin-color. Even when confronted with intergroup conflict and hostility, Blacks showed remarkable resilience and adaptation by developing their own communities and social structures to include Black churches, resource centers, educational institutions, business companies, as well as political, professional, and community organizations.

In addition, they learned to conduct effective business with dominant White society, essentially becoming highly skilled at negotiation all the while developing impressive strategies for adapting to life under the threat or dangers of White supremacy. But Whites felt Blacks had become self-serving and arrogant. So, in many cases, Whites revolted against them by massacring entire communities, sometimes moving from town-to-town in deliberate and violent killing sprees.

Today, the new excuse from White people is Blacks are inherently violent. They make White people feel discomfort, uneasiness, and fear in their presence. Some White people are genuinely concerned about the plight and predicament of Black people but believe they put themselves in their present situation by lacking ambition.

On the other hand, there are people who feel like many of today's Black folk exist in a state of learned hopelessness. The constant fact of Blacks being oppressed by White people make them feel powerless. So, life is constantly working out for White people. They continue to traumatize Blacks by thwarting their efforts to succeed in life. How is it done? That's a good question!

Whites continue to discount Black people's attempt to escape or avoid their situation, even when alternatives are ambiguously presented. So, after Blacks experience repeated overload, conflict, and frustration, many can no longer cope, frustration occurring when Blacks cannot reach their goal. The amount of stress becomes so intense and prolonged that constant failure beyond their control leads to learned hopelessness.

It is the persistent failure to succeed at life that causes many of the underlying problems we see in Black people. Persistent failure usually leads people down the slippery road to alcoholism, drug abuse, even criminal violence is associated with the inability to avoid aversive stimuli experienced beyond one's control. Depression is the typical outcome.

We saw in our discussion of why contemporary Black expressions offend White people, oppression is the ultimate reason for both positive and negative manifcstations. Blacks are confronted with chronic living conditions that include poverty, racism, and racial supremacy. It is important for people to turn their attention to White people and their daily hassles as it provides a more focused look at why contemporary Black expressions offend them so and, better, how we can work together to resolve the problem of White supremacy.

What We Can Do About It

What we can do to ultimately resolve the problem of White supremacy is turn our attention to the daily hassles of Whites. It will provide a more focused look at why contemporary Black expressions offend them so. But, in order to do so, we need to better understand White supremacy. White supremacy is structured on three important bases.

First, White supremacy is predicated on antiblack racism. White supremacists actually exacerbate their problems by acknowledging negative characteristics of Black people, containing both real and imaginary aspects of their racial identity. What this does is structure any group of emotionally significant ideas that are completely or partly repressed. The level of repression causes intrapsychic conflict leading to aggression or negative outward behavior. The result is it reinforces the negative perception that all Black people are inherently bad. This way of thinking ignores the tragedy of Black Americans, the over-glorified and often distorted history of White people, and the global presence of African and other indigenous people throughout world history.

The thinking strategies of Whites, in general, allow them to consider themselves to exist as victims in a degenerate society overtaken by Blacks and other degenerate nonwhites. In this way, the interactions that occur between Whites and Blacks, young and older, both student and professional, personal and public, are considered to be dangerous, having potentially disturbing consequences. Such old-school thinking gives way to the stereotypical belief that Black people are all the same.

Second, White supremacists have unrealistic expectations. White supremacist ideology is full of grandeur, especially delusional thinking in holding false beliefs or judgments about Black people despite incontrovertible evidence to the contrary. Their perception ignores the current state of affairs and places unrealistic demands on Black people to exist accordingly. The message it sends to the remaining public is that Blacks cannot function accordingly thus are brutish, shiftless, immoral degenerates who will likely cause harm to other people.

Poor perception places people under the false impression that White people follow a path of righteousness while condemning Blacks and others who struggle to overcome their situation here in America. So, when White extremism gains traction at a turning point in a country's history (like while former President Barack Obama was in office), it's essentially because Blacks appear to be progressing. And, Black progress brings about a state of greater vulnerability to Whites. It also reinforces to Blacks the idea that any display of ambition on their behalf is unappreciated. That level of rejection or social resistance leads to emotional overload, conflict, and frustration. The combination of the three can and more often leads to stress among Black people. And, after an intense and prolonged history of White supremacy in America, Blacks lose the ability to cope. Thus, depression sets in, manifesting as emotional trauma in Black women and aggression for Black men.

Third, White supremacists believe they are the real victims of America. Many of them feel misunderstood to the point of victimization. They believe Black people are getting undue attention from the government and at the expense of White people in America. They also believe that Affirmative Action policies create frustrating situations that place White people on an unequal playing field. They feel that Whites have to unify as a race in order to succeed in life while Black people simply cry wolf. President Joe Biden alluded to the fact that if Black people continue to ask for help when it is not needed, the government will be less inclined to assist them when help is truly needed. So, he suggested that Black people become someone else's burden.

What the government refuses to acknowledge is there is a considerable amount of frustration and anxiety among Black people. Black people lost the essential features of their culture like the Black economy, their community, and a code of moral conduct. Moreover, these essential features are not being replaced by those of the larger society. The result is poor Black people become disorganized and unsupportive of acculturating people who are nonwhite.

More often, White supremacy is modeled on myths and misconceptions about Black people. The call to duty or arms is a confession that White people are racist and xenophobic in their beliefs about Blacks. Other identity groups that jump on the racist bandwagon perpetuate much of the stereotypes and propaganda rather than informing the remaining public about the realities of racism.

The basis of White supremacy is deeply rooted in a frustration and the inability to accept change. Such conservatism often means self-imposed withdrawal from interacting with nonwhites. If possible, it also means Whites will exercise their rights or power to tease apart Blacks and other unacceptable identity groups from the beliefs and practices of mainstream culture.

As you can see, White supremacy can manifest itself through a variety of contexts. Here, it places blame on Black people who are consistently blamed for a lot of the wrongdoings in American society and for all the wrong reasons. In the next chapter, I will attempt to recorrect a few cultural discrepancies associated with Black people. The way Blacks express themselves awaits you in Chapter 2.

A Manner of Expression

Chapter 2
The Way We Express Ourselves

Southern trees bearing strange fruit
Blood on the leaves and blood at the roots
Black bodies swinging in the southern breeze
Strange fruit hanging from the poplar trees

Strange Fruit by Billie Holiday (1939)

Many African Americans stand, walk, dance
and communicate in gestures that set them
apart. Some of these movements express the
marks of blackness—liberation, creativity,
improvisation and self-determination—from
the time of slavery to now.

Smithsonian

In a manner of expression, the way Blacks behave scares a lot of people. It scares people not because they are violent by nature, but because their contemporary expressions show what type of people they are, what they are all about, and who they are to become. The way they express themselves can cause endearing feelings of affection or fondness as in a display of gratitude or solidarity. Or, their expressions can cause or make someone feel discomfort, uneasiness, and fear.

Black folk express themselves by way of gesture, behavior, and representation in art or drama. Typically, their expressions convey meaning in a symbolic way. Some of them express themselves through the arts. Others express themselves through culture. Still, more Black people express themselves in other symbolic ways.

Soul food is a culinary style cuisine that originated in the Southern regions of the United States. During antebellum, it was prepared and eaten by enslaved Africans. Today, soul food, prepared with love and affection, speaks to their survivability. As Black Americans, it is an expression of gratitude and appreciation for the small mercies that enabled many to survive the overwhelming pressures of stress and oppression. During the days of chattel slavery, many families were immediately separated as part of the indoctrination process. The few families that were left intact—and family members who were lucky enough to reunite afterward—found solace in cooking.

After slavery or throughout racial segregation, many Blacks were left destitute. For some, cooking was the only way they could afford to express their love and appreciation for family. Greens, beans, yams, sweet corn eaten directly off of the cob, hush-puppies, cornbread, johnny-cakes, breaded-stuffing, and cornmeal used as a coating for frying fish, chicken, and pork, quickly became the main staples of their meals.

Fish was a free meal for some Blacks. They say if you give a man a fish, he can eat a meal. But if you teach him how to fish, he can eat for a lifetime. One only needed to know how to fish to feed an entire family. Some plantation owners allowed Blacks to raise chickens too. Chickens were plentiful. A few chickens today could produce eggs tomorrow. As for pork, plantation owners only ate portions of the pig considered healthy. So, they would often leave scraps behind for the dogs. The ribs, feet and tail and, often, pig intestines were considered uneatable for civilized people. So, Blacks were often left with the challenge of fighting the dogs over scraps. And, there were plenty of nights where they were left hungry.

Many slaves were lucky enough to have modest gardens growing in the backyard of shacks or sheds on the plantation where they lived after they labored. Black-eyed peas were among the few rations they were allowed to grow in the garden. So, it quickly made its way to the dinner table.

At the time of emancipation, black-eyed peas were said to be lucky. The peas were said to be such good luck, it brought an end to slavery. After the Civil War (1865), Black-eyed peas would be eaten on the first day of January in commemoration of the emancipation proclamation, a public announcement written into law by President Abraham Lincoln (January 1, 1863).

To this day, black-eyed peas continue to be a tradition among Black families in the American South. In fact, the tradition of eating black-eyed peas is so impactful to the American people, it eventually became the official stable of the New Year's celebration. Soul food changed the dynamics of homes across the Southern regions of America. What we know today as Southern comfort food is a variation of soul food cooked by White Southerners. Surprised? Well, who do you think it was who taught the Southern bell how to cook Southern comfort meals? Cooking was an activity performed by Aunt Jemima, also known as Mammy. After mammy's cooking, the American South would never be the same.

Soul food also serves as a symbolic gesture for Blacks. It is a commemoration celebrating those ancestors who paved the way so the younger generation of Blacks could succeed.

Paving The Way

Over the years, many people paved the way for Blacks to progress, not only on the world stage of music entertainment, but in every facet of life. Blacks pay respect to those who came before to show admiration and deference toward the very people who made their lives possible.

Today, many recording artists in the African diaspora continue to contribute to the worldwide progression of Blacks through music entertainment and civil rights activism. They continue to fight for the independence of Africans formerly colonized by Europeans. Yet, this book is not about their success or their awards, acclaims, and accomplishments, at least, not solely.

This book concentrates greatly on Black Americans who were formerly concentrated in Africa. It shows great appreciation for the achievements and contributions of a people who continue to overcome great adversity in the face of overwhelming stress and oppression.

The manner in which Blacks convey their thoughts tell a story that evokes emotion in others. It is a highly expressive or meaningful and unique way of showing world cultures their existence.

Blacks often make their thoughts and feelings known to the world. When they cannot voice their concerns outwardly or publicly, Blacks gesture through their actions, representation in art, dance, drama, or in other symbolic ways. The look on people's faces after being influenced by the emotional content of their music, a heart-rending expression of sorrow displayed by others after examining their artwork, or a word or phrase that communicates an idea commonly expressed among or is unique to Black people, the way they express themselves sets them apart from others, making Black people special and noteworthy.

Black Americans continue to impact sophisticated society through symbolic means. Symbolisms speak volumes to their existence under the trope of sophisticated society. For example, Blacks created every genre of music known to Western culture. That's right, all of it! There are no ifs, ands, or buts about it. From the basic rhythm of the marching band to ragtime, Jazz, and rock'n roll, plus every music genre in between, Black people are the chief creators of music entertainment.

People like Little Richard, Fats Domino, and before them, Sister Rosetta Tharpe was responsible for creating iconic music. For some, it was a way for them to voice their thoughts and concerns openly or publicly.

Billie Holiday introduced the racially charged protest song Strange Fruit to the world in 1939. It was an emotional tribute to the lynching of Blacks in the American

South. Some people said Billie made a hasty and emotional decision to sing the song. That she had no self-discipline or respect for others. As emotional or inconsiderate as it may have been, for Billie, the song Strange Fruit was a strategic move to awaken a great nation to the threat of its ugly xenophobic resentment.

Harry Belafonte died an American singer, songwriter, political activist, and actor. American singer, songwriter, and pianist, Nina Simone turned to civil rights activism early in her career. She spoke out publicly in pursuing a political end to racial bigotry. She expressed her thoughts and concerns about the pain and distress her people endured under the tyranny of racial oppression.

While we're on the topic, let's take another sophisticated look at Blacks through the music recording industry. The year was 1983, and Michael Jackson performed his hit song, Billie Jean, in commemoration of Motown's greatest recording artists. Motown 25: Yesterday, Today, and Forever would be Michael's first time performing his pop tune in front of an audience of 47 million. It would also be the first time he would perform his signature dance move, the Moonwalk. What happened next would change the course of world history.

My eyes were glued to the television, mind enthralled over Michael's musical performance. His singing captivated the hearts and souls of countless millions while he mesmerized the audience with his flagrant and dramatic dance moves. It was the first time the world witnessed such dance feats. Michael Jackson moved rhythmically to Billie Jean. His never-before-seen dance style was almost magical as his sophisticated moves would soon catapult him into international stardom.

That night, Michael Jackson moved like a dancing machine. He also appeared to be gliding across water, backward, as he introduced the Moonwalk to the world. Now, I'm not sure who among the millions watched the music entertainment that night, but Phil Collins had to be among the spectators.

Phil Collins, a recording legend in the popular world of music entertainment, was profoundly influenced by Michael Jackson's Billie Jean performance. He had to be! His hit song, I Can't Dance, gave rise to Michael in a way that showed the world how special and noteworthy he was. A point scored for Black people across America, at the end of Phil Collins' music video (I Can't Dance), he paid homage to Michael Jackson in a funny and humorous dance attempt to emulate the pop star's rhythmic genius. Michael Jackson, a music icon, has been emulated by countless millions ever since.

The way Blacks express themselves tells the story of how an oppressed people continue to win in the fight against racial oppression. Both vocally and rhythmically, the way Blacks express themselves through music is a prime example of how a people can affect positive change while existing in an oppressive state. Heck, even endogenous people often disrupted attempts of colonization by using drums to communicate messages from one village to another. They also communicated messages through the use of smoke signals. They would communicate messages miles apart and in an instance by using both techniques. Drumming was, perhaps, the first form of mass communication, Morse code (Morse language code invented by Samuel F. B. Morse 1830's), the second.

Gestures Of Solidarity
Among Black Americans

Many Blacks function in ways that set them apart from others. From the days of chattel slavery to present, the way Blacks express themselves stand out as obvious expressions of blackness. For example, Blacks have a profoundly dominant walk. Some people call it be-bopping or just bopping. Others called it strutting, stud-walking, or styling. The rhythmic way Blacks walk, almost as if dancing to music, is further testament to them having confidence in their own ability to thrive in the face of overwhelming oppression. Ever heard the term, "happy-go-lucky Negro?" Well, it refers to how cheerfully unconcerned about the future Black people appeared. White people were impressed that Black men had a relaxed attitude about life even though their future appeared grim. Although they were made to endure segregation and other forms of hardship, to use the term loosely, they took life in stride, coexisting with a certain swag.

Yes, they've taken another derogatory term (swag) and turned it into a positive expression. Today, when wearing fashion that stands out as artistic, in an idiosyncratic way, Blacks call it swag or swaging. Swaging is a style of dressing followed by a creative, distinct, or artistic way of walking. However, it should not be mistake for early British usage: money or goods taken by a thief or burglar.

Many people have some expression of swag be it the way they stand, walk, dance, or communicate. The English show swag in their appearance. Vest coats worn underneath tweed jackets accented by pocket watches, plaid ties, and monogrammed glasses. English gentlemen even walk in a sophisticated and elegant fashion, showing their swag in a style they call dapper. But what sets Black people apart from others is unmistakable.

Black people use gestures in distinct ways, especially to express meaning or emotion, or to communicate their intentions without the use of words. Gestures can be expressed as subtle and indirect forms of communication and are often said to be expressed with vibrancy and confidence. In this way, Blacks are part of a complex and powerful system of communication. They often use that system to convey important messages.

Certain gestures show solidarity, especially among Blacks. These gestures have unique ties that bind them together. Or, it may manifest through selfless support for collective interests that create shared experiences. Solidarity raises the level of awareness for Blacks. It often leads them to take responsibility for supporting their own people. Many even become vested in the Black struggle out of respect not for themselves but their people. Blacks also learn to recognize the concept of community in this way.

Recognition creates a bind that strengthens Black ties to family. Many Blacks who develop a feeling of solidarity learn to see family as people with a connected history or shared experiences. This understanding raises the level of awareness yet again; and, Blacks develop respect for all the people who descend from common ancestry.

For Blacks, hand gestures are used as a symbol of solidarity, strength, defiance, and determination. One gesture defied the odds only to remain at the center of Black solidarity: the dap. The fist dap is a light pounding of interchanging fists between two or more people. Over the years, the name changed from the fist dap to a fist pound and from the fist pound, it morphed into the fist bump, which the world witnessed when Michelle Obama made the gesture to her husband, Barrack Obama, who was a senator and a US Presidential candidate. I'm not sure whether other hand gestures evolved from the fist dap or vice versa. But, the fist dap or fist bump is one defining marker that sets Blacks apart from all others.

Many people adopt Black hand gestures, ranging from the high-five to the hand-jive and then to the simple yet sophisticated fist bump. But it fails to have as great an impact as when showcased by Blacks. There is a spiritual or emotional connection that occurs whenever Blacks show solidarity through gestures or body language. The display of mutual affection highlights close bonds that exist between them. And, that's what other people fail to understand. It's not a simple showcasing of pride and joy for Blacks. It is a showing of refinement and concern for higher or greater consciousness in life.

Today, much of America uses Black hand gestures to show solidarity. But there are strong similarities in other cultures. In European cultures, for example, tipping the hat down with just enough movement is a courtesy or show of respect for women. But a quick tilt of the head up, or a quick slap and firm grip of the hand, or even exchanging fist bumps are friendly gestures, usually displayed by Black males. The up nod is a form of acknowledgment and show of respect in that you recognize or understand someone's struggles. The hand-grip and shake or, simply, the grip is often used to bring people together after a lengthy separation. The fist dap is an acknowledgment that you're in good company. It can also substitute for appraisal or approval for a job well done, much like the high-five.

You can also use gestures to dismiss a person's intentions. Blacks use gestures to show contempt, condemnation, disapproval, and annoyance for their oppressors. It also communicates a thought or feeling indirectly and without words. For example, when the government does something disapproving, Blacks telegraph their annoyance with a frown, sometimes called mugging.

At other times, gestures can give advance notice of intentions, especially unwittingly to an opponent. For example, in an attempt to hide his disapproval for Governor and Presidential candidate Rick Perry, President Barack

Obama unwittingly telegraphed his intentions in a press conference. Obama grimaced at the gesture of Rick Perry's brash behavior toward his Presidential opponents. The gesture shows how hard it is for people to micromanage their thoughts or feelings. Black people ultimately learn to communicate their intentions without uttering a word hence the term, "If looks could kill." Their gestures often create solidarity among the oppressed.

A Bond of Mutual Affection

Gestures are where Blacks develop solidarity or mutual trust in people who share their sensibilities. It is a living testament of their resilience, responsiveness, and adaptation over time. There is no one person or people more competent at expressing themselves than Blacks.

Malcolm X appealed to the sensitivity of Blacks through public speaking. He amassed such a following that at the height of the civil rights movement, his following darkened the Chicago streets for miles with angry demonstrators who disapproved of how law enforcement treated a community member while in police custody. If looks could kill, the Chicago police department would be dead. Yet Blacks, an oppressed people, showed mercy to the police by not attacking them at the slightest sign of human indecency. Brother Malcolm turned the angry crowed away after the community member received medical attention at his request.

"If looks could kill" is a metaphorical expression not necessarily associated with physical death but great disapproval or disappointment for the situation at-hand. Blacks can tell an entire story based on gestures or physical expressions. Gestures are the way they expressed themselves after centuries of enduring racial oppression. Even though White supremacy threatens their existence, the way they move their head and hands, the way they grimace or smile, the way they walk or move their bodies are prime examples of how they express themselves.

Laquesha's head-rolling and finger-waving shows how upset she is over the entire situation: If only looks could kill. The fact that a people can be oppressed and then continue to show their humanity tells that tragic story of the human condition. Yet, the humanity of Blacks will not allow them to act out, physically, against the very people who cause them great misery: but if only looks could kill.

People follow a course of conduct. It's usually their path in life that leads them apart. Some people take the high road in life while others take the low road. Although, the low road often exerts a heavy toll for those who walk its path.

It appears White people have taken the low road, a dark and menacing path to achieving enlightenment. In the process, they rape, pillage, and blunder world cultures. Slavery, eugenics, and segregation, each of these social systems were created to advance White civilization. And while White people prosper from oppressing Blacks, strangers, and others, many lose the ability to experience compassion for those they feel are not the same. On the other hand, the tyranny of oppression strengthens the human condition or the human will. Remember, it was Friedrich Nietzsche who said, "What doesn't kill you will make you stronger."

The Weight of Humanity

Oppression is too much for one person to bear. So, an entire race must bear the burden or the weight of humanity for the rest of the world. Colonization is a test of the human condition or the human will. It's where the oppressed learn to teach compassion, benevolence, or humility to their oppressors. A demonstration on civil disobedience led to the systemic abuse of countless others during America's civil rights movement.

Mohandas Karamchand Gandhi led his people in a political protest against British colonialism. He opposed the political orientation that advocated aggressive extension of authority over India. During one particular demonstration, the British fired countless rounds of ammunition into a crowed of demonstrators. In the aftermath, three hundred demonstrators lay dead in the streets. The British counted the loss of life a victory for British colonialism. Gandhi also considered the demon-stration a victory but for his people. The demonstration showed how inhumane or uncompassionate the British were.

Kindness, compassion, and humility are the tools of humanity, the high road to achieving enlightenment. It is through their humanity people develop compassion for others. Their humanity prevents them from showing inhumanity toward strangers and others.

What We Can Do About It

What we can do here is instigate social change in thinking strategies. Whites are often resistant to the idea of change because they fear social competition. Blacks have always been considered a competition group by Whites. So, if one was to begin with the threat of social competition, then understand there is a *psychology of victimization* present—a form of oppression whereby one or more competition groups are singled out for cruel or unjust treatment. Black people have been oppressed by Whites for more than five hundred years due to the prominent history they had in Europe. But their hopes can be recovered. There can be a psychology of change.

Newer or younger generations need to be a part of the psychology in order to promote this school of thought. Like any unpleasant feeling caused by fear, the perceived threat of danger, pain, or harm poisons the mind and creates a situation whereby people feel exempt from liability, duty, or obligation. In this way, the cultural mainstream will refuse to accommodate Blacks, strangers, and others.

For centuries, the cultural mainstream refused to accommodate Blacks in fear of who they are, what they are all about, and the future in which they are headed. The cruel or harsh treatment Blacks endure changes the way they express themselves.

Today, they are an outspoken, very vocal racial group. Their communication skills baffle the cultural mainstream. Many of their expressions are idiosyncratic in nature. But when confronting the cultural mainstream, many are erudite and can turn any discussion into a political debate.

Now, I do understand the psychology of competition groups and why most societies refuse to accommodate strangers and others. But people can learn to coexist. In order for people to coexist, there has to be a change in thinking strategies. There must be a psychology of change. But the question remains, how do we promote a version of psychology that instigates social change, and for all?

First, we must reduce the amount of discomfort, uneasiness, and fear associated with accommodating strangers and others. Why? Forming new relationships more often means we must accommodate the needs or wishes of others. We must also ensure people understand that accommodation does not mean sacrifice. Most of the time, accommodation means making others feel comfortable in their new environment.

To begin this process, people need to be educated or well-informed on race, ethnicity, culture, and nationality. This doesn't necessarily mean they have to receive a formal education, either. The process is as easy as picking up a book and reading it. Or, people can become part of a congregation dedicated to the learning and spreading of contemporary information.

People who are socially resistant to change more often avoid forming new relationships. The problem is we find aversion in people resistant to change. We also find aversion in people who hold conservative attitudes. Conservatives hold steadfast to the idea of tradition. That way, they can avoid specific schools of thought in fear of change, especially abrupt change.

Both types of social phobias (i.e., aversion and conservatism) affect how we respond to people in the real world. So, people averse to change are phobic and will avoid developing new relationships. Dually noted: There is no place in human society for anyone who is phobic toward progressive change. So, the idea is to bring people into a new age of enlightenment. Both education and information can help reduce the amount of social resistance that create discomfort, uneasiness, and fear of change or dare I say, fear of Black people.

Actually, what we are talking about is extinguishing the prejudiced nature of people to reduce the amount of racial tension that keeps them from developing healthy intergroup relationships. Prejudice is not extinguished by enacting common laws or imposing complex consequences of law, but through the use of education or information. An underline pathway must lay at the core in order to instigate social change.

What I am trying to say is there must be a sequence of changes or events occurring if intergroup relations are to constitute real progression. This psychology of change could be more productive if pushed through the use of politics. But, it is just as affective if we were to generate a sense of duty or service from the public. Both education and information are tools used to reduce racial tension and hostility between cultural groups. Both work to reduce political resistance rooted in a bitter history. Call it a type of conscience, both guiding pathways lead to a psychology of change.

Certainly, a psychology of change must be multi-faceted if it is to work. It needs to target every facet of community life not only to include the cultural mainstream but identity groups that are not considered competition. This school of thought must include groups left out of the equation and those having no stake in the game. And the process needs to start at the grassroots level.

Blacks are the most segregated racial group in American society. They're more often ignored by the cultural mainstream. We need to push for sensitivity training in politics and other areas of common interest to reduce the amount of fear that commonly associates them as a competition group. The amount of education or information will teach people to have respect and consideration for Blacks, strangers, and others. In this way, we reduce the amount of prejudice and bigotry that forces nonwhites into an oppressive or a cruel and harsh state.

The idea behind a psychology of change is not for us to make competition groups appear docile or submissive in the eyes of the beholder. No, we're not trying to create more minority (subordinate) groups nor should the way groups express themselves be a measure of resilience, responsiveness, or adaptation over time. In fact, we're trying to preserve a national heritage by doing away with a culture of hatred that victimizes nonwhite identity groups.

A psychology of change is not a political tool used to wipe out entire histories. Instead, it is an effort to bring a critical part of history, culture, and heritage into awareness so people will not have to express themselves so differently as to appear completely new. A psychology of change is forth-right yet humbling. It has the ability to take xenophobic threats that come from discomfort, uneasiness, and fear and then reduce it down to an utterance of nonsense. A psychology of change is a chance to guide society by its moral conscience.

In the next chapter, we will explore certain aspects of moral conscience. The fact that Blacks have always been guided by their moral conscience awaits you in chapter 3.

Chapter 3
To be Guided

A Manner of Expression

White people have taken a dark and menacing path to achieving enlightenment. I find it rather ominous that they have yet to resolve the problem of racism and White supremacy. The people who hold power and control the institutions in American society are, today, a proven source of danger or harm to Blacks. No longer can Black folk afford to ignore the cruel, harsh, or ruthless treatment they endure at the hands of their oppressors. The time is now for Blacks to be guided by their conscience.

McGuire in press

In this day and age—when the American government is following a grim and immoral path to achieve the status of world leader—dominant White society has proven it is a source of danger or harm to Black folk. Blacks must fortify themselves against the potential threat of suffering harm or injury. In order to fortify themselves against all odds, they must understand the rightness or wrongness of their own conduct or motives. Thus, the time has come for Black people to be guided by their conscience.

In a sense, Black people have always been guided by their moral conscience. It's what helped them attempt to civilize Europeans at the end of antiquity (711AD). And, it's what helped them to survive chattel slavery.

Your *conscience*—a moral sense of right and wrong behavior—exists as a guiding principle. It governs both your thoughts and actions. It's the main psychological protective mechanism that forces you into your own sense of right and wrong or good and bad conduct, or healthy and poor decisions. When you experience shame after doing something immoral, it's because your conscience forces you to conform to your own sense of right conduct. Most people adhere to a code of conduct we consider right or acceptable. Largely, your conscience is an extraordinary sense of your moral character.

To be guided by your conscience is not a simple showcasing of pride and joy. In fact, it is a showing of refinement and understanding for higher or greater awareness in life. There are two main paths one can travel to attain a sense of moral conscience. The path of virtue (the high road) is a work of great merit. It is a motivation that comes chiefly from developing a sense of moral reasoning. Whether we derive our conscience from establishing a sense of ethics (based chiefly on logic) or moral reasoning, your guiding conscience will manifest your thoughts and actions toward a greater awareness of life.

Then there is the path of immorality (the low road). White people, in taking a dark and menacing path to achieving enlightenment, have taken a page from the dark and disenchanted history of Europe. They are seemingly unconcerned about what's right, fair, or just. They only show imperial interests in extending authority over foreign territories. Such a political orientation is not concerned with standards of right or good conduct. As a result, human society considers their sophisticated ways of living to be morally objectionable.

For example, American prisons are part of the criminal justice system. Unfortunately, the prison system is rooted in American slavery. It is a form of property owning, which includes involuntary servitude accepted as punishment for crimes committed under penalty of law. While serving as Governor of Arkansas, former President William Jefferson (Bill) Clinton partook in an indentured servitude program in his state. Most, if not all of his servants were criminals who served out their prison sentences working for Clinton at the Governor's mansion. To this very day, he's made no qualms about his role in the exploitation of incarcerated Blacks working as indentured servants in his home state.

Today, there are more Black males existing in American prisons than at the height of US slavery. Currently, there are two-point-four million Black males, increasingly females, existing in what we know as the industrial prison complex. And with the privatizing of American prison systems, an increasing number of Blacks will be bartered or traded off as slave labor. Many incarcerated Blacks will be forced to work for cheap wages comparable to incomes found in third world or developing countries.

Most American laws were enacted to protect Whites and their civil liberties. However, many people are concerned that these laws (the ones governing our prison systems and other institutions) encroach on human rights. Human rights violations range from state-sponsored murder and domestic terrorism to false incarceration and from Eugenics or human experimentation to institutional-ization where people often suffer the deleterious effects of long-term residence. Granted, only a few states have instituteionalization policies in place. But, such discussions are more of a reality since the Supreme Court overturned the historical landmark decision Roe *v.* Wade.

What the overturning of Roe *v.* Wade means is that beyond sex discrimination, the government can now legally infringe on your God given freedoms, human rights, and civil liberties. For example, encroaching on your right to privacy will no longer be considered a civil rights violation.

The Roe *v.* Wade decision not only protected women's rights, it protected the 9th and 14th amendments. The 14th Amendment says, in part, that no state can deny to any person within its jurisdiction equal protection under the law. Title IX specifically prohibits sex discrimination.

The 9th amendment states that the rights of the people are not limited to what is written or listed in the United States Constitution. That whatever rights not listed in the US Constitution also belongs to the people, not just the US government. The systemic abuse of Black people pretty much sums up the new experience in America. In other words, widespread systemic abuse like discrimination, institutionalization, eugenics, and increased poverty will occur even for White people with the overturning of Roe *v.* Wade.

White people have no conscience about their cruelty. The term Make America Great Again (MAGA) is living testament to just how profound their cruelty is. Many Republican supporters are conservative. They would like to restore American society to an earlier time (1956 – 1957) when White people benefitted from White-only policies and government programs. Housing lending programs, White-only work policies, even public assistance, ironically, was a time when White people felt they were distinguished and worthy. Yes, many of them believed themselves to be considerably superior, regarded collect-ively.

Nuclear, biological, and chemical warfare (NBC) is also a testament to their cruelty. It was the Germans who introduced poisonous gas to the world. On April 22, 1915, German forces, fighting along the Western front, fire over one hundred fifty tons of lethal chlorine gas at two French allied colonial forces held up in Ypres, Belgium. It was the first known gas attack in the world. The Germans used chemical weapons to kill enemy combatants. It devastated the allied front. But it was Americans who introduced the atomic bomb to the world.

America detonated not one but two atomic bombs over Japan. The Japanese cities of Hiroshima and Nagasaki were brutally destroyed. America killed an estimated eighty thousand people, largely Japanese citizens, with tens of thousands more later dying from radiation exposure.

Although weapons of mass destruction are, today, said to be too inhumane to use, superpowers such as Russia and the United States continue to find unique and destruct-ive ways unleash their wrath on counties that challenged their authority.

Man's inhumanity toward man explains much of the misery and suffering found in the world. It seems that

White people are innately inhumane. Perhaps because their race has yet to fully evolve, they lack and reflect the lack of humanity needed to show compassion toward others. Without compassion for misery or suffering (as I believe Whites are Cro-Magnon), is it even fair for them to speak on their humanity in the presence of nonwhites? James Baldwin once said:

> I imagine one of the reasons White people cling to their hates so stubbornly is because they sense, once hate is gone, they will be forced to deal with pain.

James Baldwin assumed that White aggression was not psychopathic in nature. His reasoning may have very well evolved from him dealing with the overwhelming pressure of stress and oppression. His attempts to reason with White hatred, even after enduring the traumatic experience of racism, one can only conclude James Baldwin was guided by his conscience.

Interestingly, it does seem to be a painstaking process for White people to resolve their hatred of Blacks. For them, it seems to be a privilege, a sense of entitlement they hold near or dear to their hearts. The pain they fear, as Baldwin so eloquently suggested, will come from the threat or fear of losing their sense of entitlement, assuming Blacks gain economic advantage. The use of oppression keeps White people from fearing they will one day be subjugated and made to endure hardship by the very people they oppress. That's why so many Whites have a desire to fight or flee. And although Whites make excuses for their aggression, using statements like "I fear for my life," many are referencing their own feelings of implicit hate.

They say Odin, ruler of Aesir, developed a profound sense of knowledge and wisdom through continuous war. He achieved great virtue for which he gave his eye. Supreme God of war or Wotan, Odin developed a sustained enthusiasm for poetry, knowledge, and wisdom.

White people have not lost or sacrificed one iota of privilege or ounce of pride to achieve the wisdom necessary to establish healthy intergroup relationships with Blacks or any other group of people on this planet. It would seem to me that what they did learn was or is to respect self-serving values. Proof can be found written in the pages of the United States Declaration of Independence. Perhaps, the most important words written in the Declaration of Independence, Life, Liberty, and the pursuit of Happiness is a reference hinting at putting one's own wellness and interests ahead of others.

As a custom, Whites turned individualism into a cultural practice. It is a cultural-based belief that, in a civilized society, individuals can succeed in life if they pull themselves up by their bootstraps. This belief implies that Western and Northern societies are meritocratic. While meritocracy has its strong points, it does have a few drawbacks.

Meritocracy centers on the belief that only those having superior intellect should have and be able to rule by way of international or political influence and military power. On the same token, people who follow this belief system strongly believe their leaders should be chosen for their superior abilities and not because of their wealth, status, or birthright. A bit of a conundrum, I know! It does make sense, right? We've already experienced the zany antics of former President Donald Trump and his White House staff of chums or cronies. Donald Trump was able to secure a place in global history simply because he is a plutocrat. Whether he was actually qualified to perform his political duties, until this day, remains to be seen. But what we did witness was Trump personally benefitting under his presidential administration.

Also known as the title of Nobility Clause, Article I, Section 9, Clause 8 of the US Constitution prohibits anyone in government office from accepting gifts, emolument, office, or a title from royalty or foreign states without congressional consent. In fact, no president is allowed to personally profit, be it monetary or economic gain, while holding public office. Yet, Donald Trump did such largely through the use of his estate: Mar-a-Lago club, a resort in Palm Beach, Florida. His profits were said to have reached as high as one-hundred-forty million dollars during his time as Commander-in-Chief.

What a paradox! On the one hand, we would like for our nation's leaders to show intelligence and competence. On the other hand, their intelligence doesn't ensure they will behave accordingly. President Joe Biden already serves as an example as he repeatedly tried to turn his back on Black folk, the people who placed him in

Office. In an interview with Charlamagne Tha God, broadcasted on "The Breakfast Club," Presidential candidate Joe Biden said, if you don't vote for him, then you're not Black. Yet, after less than 100 days in office, Biden said he did enough for Blacks and expected them to support other racial groups that were benefitting from better support in society. And, Donald Trump already serves as a prime example of what happens when people vote under a system of buffoonery. So, trust is the paradox at-hand.

Unflagging Conscience

To truly express themselves, Blacks must be people of unflagging conscience. At a time when public speaking could very well end your existence, Blacks must be marked by firm determination. Malcolm X was steadfast in his convictions. He was a stalwart supporter and a devout Muslim from the Nation of Islam. He stood by the principles of democracy until the very end of his existence.

Even after Brother Malcolm felt that the Nation of Islam betrayed him, he did not violate his principles. What he did do was open a place of prayer for him and his following, one separate from the Nation of Islam. There, at the Boston Temple of Ministry: Muslim Mosque Number 11, he continued practicing the Islamic faith. Then on that tragic day, Malcolm died a man of principle. Malcolm X was assassinated on February 21, 1965 while delivering a public lecture at the Audubon Ballroom in Washington Heights, Manhattan, New York City.

Reverend Martin Luther King, Jr. also died standing by his principles. So did Marcus Garvey, Medga Evers, Kwame Ture (Stokely Carmichael), and many other important Black public figures in American history. Black women leaders like Fannie Lou Hamer and Barbara Jordan acted in accordance with morality. They were profoundly principled. Ida B. Wells-Barnett was assassinated at the age of 63 for campaigning against public lynchings. She was principled. Ida was murdered by her neighborhood grocery store butcher. He poisoned her with arsenic.

There are seemingly endless leaders in the Black community who were assassinated by members of the White establishment in Washington, DC. Many people who stand out as principled are targeted for assassination by a government supposedly bound by the principles of freedom and democracy or so goes the story. People, today, are no different. If you're Black and assume the role of leader in American society, you become targeted for victimization. And with a target on your back, it's only a matter of time before you are assassinated.

Throughout American history, many prominent leaders from the Black community died tragically, speaking out against the tyranny of White supremacy and racial oppression. We must be guided by the set of principles that govern our thoughts and actions. There must also be conformity to one's own sense of right or good conduct. Shame must become an intuitive part of our sensibilities such that we quickly overwhelm whenever we act immorally. In fact, we must be guided by a course or code of personal conduct.

Behaving In Principled Ways

In order for Blacks to follow a code of personal conduct, they must behave in ways that are principled. The manner in which people behave is a direct result of their conscience. In America, Blacks have been demonized and demoralized to the point that many lose their sense of spirituality. They are said to be burdensome, others menacing or troubling and, even, more are portrayed as wicked and threatening. The cultural attitude toward Blacks is so defining it caused most of them to lose confidence or hope in their own abilities. And since Black people are expected to behave poorly, many of them start believing it's a natural part of their human characteristics. So, they behave poorly and fall prey to the system of oppression.

Network television, media entertainment, and social media work to reinforce social stigmas. Blacks became infamous under the assertion that they were violent, shiftless, and lazy. Thanks to the systematic desensitization of America through network television, for a while, world cultures were made indifferent to Black suffering. After all, the world is made up of many civilizations. Unfortunately, Africa is said to be the only continent uncivilized.

It's only been recent, perhaps, since White Americans turned their backs on their nonwhite counterparts, that many people have come to realize they too are at constant risk for victimization by Whites. They try to identify with White people by passing off their appearance as White or appealing to White morality. Many nonwhites come to America hoping they can become honorary Whites.

The term *honorary White* refers to individuals and racial groups that belong to a racial hierarchy. The hierarchy starts with Whites at the top and Blacks at the bottom. People who exist between these groups are given the intermediate status of second-class citizens. These groups—some nonwhites and part-White racial groups—often try to associate with members of the dominant society to elevate their social status.

Today, even certain Asian and Latino groups in the United States are referred to as honorary Whites. The Japanese were among the first Asian groups to achieve the status of honorary Whites. As a result, many Asian groups call the Japanese the White men of Asia. And with the White population existing below the birth population rate, many of these racial groups are trying to see just where they fit in.

But in the age of consciousness, and for woke folk, many young people from these semiaccepted racial groups aren't buying into the idea of social acceptance. Today's youth are not receptive to the idea of achieving Whiteness through their social status. They see that many racial groups have experienced great cruelty by the White race. They've come to realize that while White people target

Blacks for victimization—once the Black population becomes extinct—sooner or later, other identity groups will be targeted. Young Asians try to awaken their elders to the fact that the entire motivation behind oppression is race.

However, the younger generation, young people from every walk of life, are here to tell their elders that Whiteness is not the prize. That regardless of their skin-tone, straight hair, education, or social status, being racist toward Black people will not bring them closer to achieving Whiteness. No matter what they do to gain acceptance, they will always be considered inferior to Whites. That the respect they crave from White people, and in trying to achieving the status of Whiteness, proves nothing.

The younger generation appears to be guided by their conscience. It's not just about identifying with Blacks, either. People from every walk of life are choosing to embrace their culture first. They also recognize that there is more than one ultimate principle needed to guide or govern a society. To coexist in a pluralistic society like America, we must achieve harmony among the masses. It will take some doing, though.

Black people are the most hated racial group on the planet. There has been a concerted effort by the masses to portray them as wicked and threatening. As a result, many people would like Blacks to be teased apart from mainstream society. Their goal is not to completely remove them from the planet's population but to reduce their presence to the point of unawareness. Sadly, many cultures and societies will not change its public policies to include Blacks as equal. These cultures would rather maintain their public policies in hopes of one day achieving the social status of Whiteness.

For the younger generation, their goal is to find a harmony of interest among and between separate and distinct cultural systems. But for this to happen, group-oriented cultural practices must be respected. The arts, science, religion, and other cultural progressions that make up the human intellectual achievement, should be regarded collectively and with compassion. If people learn to see strangers and others in a compassionate way, certainly respecting cultural differences, then we will begin to see that every race has contributions its members can offer. For example, Black people committed a legacy of gains to Western civilization. It is said that the only thing the White man invented was the US Patent and Trademark Office. That way, they could steal all of the inventions Black people create. Oh yes, Blacks have been very busy creating, inventing, and discovering. The problem is most certain Whites and their refusal to credit Blacks with making important contributions. They refuse to credit Blacks not only in America but throughout the world.

Do you recall earlier that Germans introduced poisonous gas to the world when they used one-hundred-fifty tons of it to kill off enemy combatants? Well, it was Garrett A. Morgan who first introduced the gas mask to the world, during World War I. In 1914, Garrett patented a breathing apparatus, which was sealed off by a canvas hood. He demonstrated its usage during a mining accident whereby coal miners were trapped in a mine by poisonous gas. The military immediately adopted Garrett's invention, today calling it the gas mask.

All military personnel undergo extensive training using Garett Morgan's invention: the gas mask. Although it has undergone major improvements, his invention has withstood the test of time. It's authentic and ingenious. It also shows the world that anyone can contribute to human society.

Speaking on the issue of ingeniousness and Black creativity, England has decided to recognize or acknowledge African American's contributions to the English language. A bit suspect, I fear their acknowledgment is another show of disrespect for Black people. Important contributions Black Americans made to the world is being overlooked by a rather simple acknowledgment of a few spoken words. Words like ain't, isn't, and don't hardly surmise the creative ingeniousness found among Black Americans, past, presence, or future. Which reminds me, you should also know that it was the Europa tribe of West Africa that is to be accredited with creating the English language. They used seven of the major European languages to create what is, today, known as the English language system. But, I digress.

Black people are not complimentary pieces of a puzzle that bring a special atmosphere to the whole of civilization. Globally and historically, they contribute a legacy of gains not just to America, but to the world. So, it is more than their presence that lends a certain cachet to Western civilization. Blacks are the people who make White civilization a Western World.

Perhaps, their historical progress is the very reason why Whites refuse to teach critical race theory (CRT) in grade school settings. In college, CRT courses are taught as an elective. So, those courses are pretty much tucked away, buried in the halls of academia. Critical Race Theory is designed to correct historical discrepancies in order to teach the totality of history. Now, I hope this passage adds a light note to the problems surrounding race matters. It is only fair for White people to assume full responsibility for the suffering of Blacks. The conservative belief of making America great again (MAGA) is a dying of old hopes for people who refuse to progress.

What We Can Do About It

How we can capture the new spirit and vision of the younger generation to ensure that the challenges of our past do not consume them is to, first, admit that our most valuable sources for hope, strength, and power lies well within ourselves. We should also connect through common interests. Then we should turn to the past in order to look for historical events that act as a basis or model from which we can learn to understand the deep psychological crisis we're in.

The next thing we can do is practice pluralism and use the method of "Each One Teach One." For example, when someone learns how to read or write or they gain knowledge in some way, it becomes their responsibility to teach someone else. The idea is for each person in your community or neighborhood to teach one person the knowledge they acquired, causing a ripple effect of information that spreads knowledge throughout the entire neighborhood, community and, eventually, across the country. Each One Teach One brings awareness to people or the situation at-hand. It also refers to cooperative learning. Cooperative learning helps people develop oral communication skills, a necessary skill-set needed to improve our ability to socially interact with others in the real world.

A lot of people from the younger generation would love to coexist. The fusion of Black samurai in Japan is exciting to many Japanese youth. China has long since accepted White Buddhists. And no one knew Asian and White Muslims were a thing until the late 1960's early 1970's. The world is vastly changing. And, people appear to be okay with it. Although, there are those who would like to keep life unchanged or, dare I say, stagnant.

Conservatives hide their discomfort, uneasiness, and fear behind social customs and tradition. Their conservative attitude leads to a culture of social resistance. And, social resistance leads to the static development of culture. With static development, there is often vast changes in technology but very little change in the cultural attitude or growth of humanity. The combination is how we develop artificial selection verses natural selection.

Next, we need to focus on our common interests. It's our common interests that lead people to embrace cultural pluralism. *Pluralism* is a system in which two or more cultures, identity groups, be it racial or ethnic, or sources of authority coexist by recognizing more than one ultimate principle. In other words, pluralism recognizes the significance of various cultures and societies coexisting as one big united front. It's literally the need to gain social acceptance that creates a pathway to wanting recognition or the need for cultural distinction by separating various cultural groups into distinct cultural systems. People should have a right to be assimilated into a given society. Pluralism gives them that option. The problem is not with assimilation but the idea of mainstream culture accommodating others.

Mainstream culture has very little regard for the wellness of nonwhites. Believe it or not, most people choose to be assimilated when they move to a new culture. However, people from the cultural mainstream often fear that their rights, privileges, or entitlements will be affected if they begin to accommodate or power share with people from developing nations. They impose laws that prevent nonwhites from achieving equal opportunity among the cultural mainstream. Confronted with those facts, how will we, as a civilization, ever come to achieve true humanity?

It's time for the younger generation to instigate social change, not only at the community and political level, but to appeal to humanity as a whole. That's right, the time has come for us to invigorate the common good of humanity. Fortunately, we do not need to look at new frameworks that provide structure and new communication methods that can produce new truths. Old truths should be able to verify, perhaps, new ways of thinking or existing in ways that instigate social change.

And last: Out of social change should emerge new leadership. New leadership should not be bothered or burdened with new frameworks intended as a guide for correcting past mistakes. Nor should they turn to political conservatism as a way to restore faith in the public. New leaders need to have a good understanding of the current historical narrative of this country and the world; so, they can address it properly. They should also embody the principles of democracy and should be able to invoke these guiding principles in ways that invigorate even the destitute or people who have no stake in the game. Only those who can bring out the best of our humanity should be considered as they are the only potential leaders worthy of rearing and encouraging.

A few of these leaders are already here and have been groomed to uphold freedom of democracy. But with old leadership making a last-ditch effort to restore the past, work is truly cut out for new leadership.

We can only hope and pray that humanity prevails. We have entire worlds built on lies, privileges, and unique opportunities stolen from the pages of history. And, they're not ready to give up their comfort without a fight. So, for those of you who are slow moving for the sake of caution, either we're led peaceably by our conscience, or as James Baldwin once quoted, it's the fire next time.

This concludes our discussion on moral conscience. In the next chapter, we will turn our attention to which behaviors cause thought-provoking concerns for White people.

Chapter 4
Thought-Provoking Concerns for White People

A Manner of Expression

Hatred is too strong an emotion to waste on someone you don't like.

Hispanic Musician (Anonymous)

Who we are, what we're all about, and who we are to become in life has thought-provoking concerns for many people. It is often a curious question to Blacks, a quite dangerous progression to others and, well, causes thought-provoking concerns for White people. The progression of Black folk speaks to their glorious past. The Moors sailed the open Seas long before their failed attempt at civilizing Whites, their current struggles against racial oppression and open bigotry, and their much-anticipated future in which there is great discomfort, uneasiness, and fear. Many people fear competent Black people. Prospects of their future, as a people, frightens the world.

The world has been conditioned to hate Blacks, Africans included. As a result, many world cultures seek to exploit, oppress, and humiliate them. In order for nonwhites to achieve the social status of Whiteness, they will make full use of Blacks and benefit off of their blood, sweat, and tears. To ensure Black servility, the United States government destroyed nearly every aspect of the Black identity. Forcing Black people to take on Eurocentric names, adopting White mannerisms, learning every aspect of European history, and destroying the Black economy ensures Black folk will conform to White cultural expectations.

But you say their free people, right? Well, let me explain freedom to you. According to the Reconstruction Amendments, that is to say, the 13th, 14th, and 15th Amendments, Blacks were given liberty, not freedom. *Freedom* is the ability to act, speak, or think without hinderance or restraints. *Liberty* is the condition of free-bound thinking so long as it does not interfere or threaten the existence of the sociopolitical hierarchy. Freedom is unbound thinking and expressing while liberty is conditional thinking used in accordance with limits set by a political hierarchy. So long as Black people conform to their cultural expectations, they're free to do is they please.

I often hear Black people ask questions like "Who are we; where did we come from; what religion were we before we were indoctrinated into Christianity?" And for many, the answers are more disturbing than not knowing.

As a people, Black Americans are historically tied to a few religions. Those who descend from the Moors have strong ties to Islam, others Hebraism, more are spiritually connected to Christianity as some Moors were allegedly Christian. Still, there were Blacks who practiced spirituality without having ties to religion. There are African nations that do not follow religion as a practice, either. And why not? Fact of the matter is religion falls under the social category of mythology. Ouch! I know. The truth hurts. And don't let religious people hear you say that. The Israelis will banish you from ever stepping foot in the country. The Arabs war with entire nations over such sayings. And, well, Christians will pray that you lose your heathenish ways and join them in the Kingdom of God, a Germanic concept.

People are forever saying the truth hurts. That ignorance is bliss. For me, *ignorance* means being in a state of perfect happiness, oblivious to everything that matters. And without knowing who you are, what your people are all about, and what you're meant to be in life is an example of living in a state of blissful ignorance. There are a lot of Black folk in the world doing just that, living in a state of total ignorance, oblivious to everything. This feeling of obliviousness is not without merit, though.

Black Americans are conditioned to hate everything about themselves to include their culture, customs, traditions and, for most, African cultural belief systems. There are many books written about Black history and each one tells their story. The problem is Black people have been conditioned to believe that books written by Black scholars are invalid. Thus, validation is the key word.

People believe that reference books written by Black scholars are invalid. They feel Black scholars are ungrateful and bitter people because their race was savage and needed saving by Whites who, by the way, civilized every aspect of the Black identity to include who they are, what they're all about, and where they came from. In addition, more people believe that Black reference books are not peer reviewed by qualified scholars, academics, or academic specialists working in academia. Fact of the matter is most reference books written by Black scholars undergo a critical process of peer review and are published by White publishing companies. There are about four thousand publishing companies in the United States. Less than one percent of the publishing companies are owned or coopted by Blacks. Penguin books, Anchors Publishing, and others like Brown & Benchmark are well-established, historically White publishing companies with notoriety and prestigious reputations. So, you can bet your bottom dollar that Black reference books have been thoroughly scrutinized before joining noted scholarly reference books on book shelves of academia.

Another reason why so many Black folk refuse to pick up a book and read is based on the fact that we've been conditioned to think reading is not a good thing to do. In fact, we've been taught to think reading is not cool. We socialize our lives as we are tactile creatures by nature. Social interaction gives us the false belief that so long as we communicate with one another, there is constant learning at work; and, that's good enough.

At one point in American history, the most educated group of Blacks congregated in churches and social clubs. The trickle-down experience was for Blacks to join the church as a form of sanctuary. The upside was what appeared to be rewards for having faith in a truth, a truth in the existence of a supreme being having power over nature or human fortunes. For the most part, this is no longer true as most Black people no longer congregate in the church.

In fact, we socialize our behaviors so much that we tend to speak figuratively. Figurative speech opens the door for colloquial expressions, slang, even Ebonics, an American form of broken English spoken by Black Americans, said to be a language in its own right rather than a dialect of standard English. As you can gather, I am not a fan of Ebonics. However, slang is such a colorful tense of informal language that many people believe it sounds cool when spoken, myself included.

Slang is an informal expression of language we use to convey our innermost thoughts and feelings. It evolved from speaking figuratively or speaking in a symbolic way. This is where Blacks learn to express themselves by way of gesture, behavior, and representation in the arts or drama. It's when Black people can say the exact same thing and get two different meanings from it. Or, Black people can say completely different things and get the same meaning simply from watching and interpreting the other person's body language, a type of code talking if you will. Similarly, switching between formal and informal language is what they've come to call code-switching.

Code-switching is the practice of alternating between two or more languages or various languages in conversation. When a person code-switches, he or she converts their primary language usually to a secondary form in a way that can be generalized to a greater audience. It can also lead to slandering words or the development of slang language.

Slang is not unique to Blacks people. It originated from people who mispronounced spoken words and phrases in public. In many countries, languages do not have certain words or letters in its communication systems. Those people often mispronounce words as a result of their awkwardness of never pronouncing certain spoken letters and words. The "R" sound in most Asian cultures is nonexistent. So, they substitute it with the "L" sound. Words like "rice" is pronounced as "lice." People ignorantly tease Asians for their inability to pronounce the "L" sound properly. If you've ever been in a fast-food Chinese restaurant and ordered the fried rice, then you know exactly what I'm talking about. In fact, you may have heard people tease Asians for the way they pronounce it: flied lice.

To make a mockery of someone causes them to appear foolish or absurd. It is the absurdities that legitimizes the hatred that divides people in American society. Mockery ridicules the person or people and sets a poor example by Americans. Who we are, what we are all about, and where we're headed in life may very well depend on how well we learn to socially interact with strangers and others.

Today, Black people use slang more than any identity group on Earth. In fact, many Blacks prefer to use slang over standard English. Why? They choose not to mimic their oppressors. That statement is true due to the fact that Blacks were psychologically and culturally removed from both their traditional societies and the larger, dominant society. And let's not talk about the feelings of alienation and identity loss that creates marginalization. Yet, Black slang is so influential and popular among its people, it more often finds its way into the homes of mainstream America.

The transition is problematic for many people. Slang is a substandard form of language. Many people feel that the use of slang will move American society from an advance stage of human social development to some degenerate form of higher civilization. For example, White children shifted away from listening to classical music like Mozart's Requiem in D minor and ballroom dancing. Today, they break-dance and listen to hip-hop music, street music created by Black and Hispanic Americans. The transition took about ten to fifteen years to make, from the 1980's to the new millennium. Part of the result was the use of words like weed and trees (Black slang) used to describe marijuana. Socializing the use of the words lead people to think smoking marijuana is okay behavior. Blacks use the coded words as a way to prevent dominant White society from understanding their intentions.

When mainstream Americans use slang, it is often distorted. In their own warped way of thinking, they attempt to normalize what they perceive to be okay language. Yes, it's sad to say that even though we exist in separate and distinct cultural systems, it is easier to pick up on the latest slang and curse words before speaking standard English language.

Yesterday, words such as "fixing" were used in slang sentences like "I'm fixing to go upside your head." Today, the word fixing morphed into "finna" as in I'm finna go upside your head." Yesterday, Blacks used the term "bro" to refer to brother. Today, they use the slur "bruh" to prevent Whites from imitating Black slang language. Using the slur "bruh" is just a hint at how words transgress beyond the limits set by moral principles. In this way, slang is a never-ending digression.

What's odd about the situation of slang or Ebonics is if Whites would offer to accommodate Blacks by absorbing them into an established mainstream, many of them would voluntarily relinquish their own identity. Instead, dominant society exercises its power to exclude Blacks from assimilating into the larger society.

From standard English to slang and from slang to Ebonics, there appears to be an erosion of languages, moral principles, standards, and laws that allow Blacks to establish their own code of conduct.

The term down-by-law refers to following principles that govern street life. Have you ever heard the saying, "There is honor among thieves." Well, that simply means there are limits of which thieves will not go beyond to steal. The same thing is true for people who live their lives by principles abound by street life. Many of them have a moral code, a code of conduct, or a street code of behavioral conduct that they believe should not be broken or betrayed. Yet for some, their code of conduct loses itself in the translation. But, basically, the rules of engagement remain the same.

From the Caribbean to North America, descendants of American slaves speak in slang. Blacks across America use slang as a standard way to convey their thoughts. As a result, dominant society feels like America will become a degenerate form of higher civilization within the next forty years. They say many identity groups are already merging to form a new society (a melting pot of degenerates who will destroy what dominant society has built). Perhaps it's the universe's way of correcting past transgressions committed by Whites. It's like fighting a losing battle. As White identity groups reduce in population, use of slang becomes more common.

In fact, Blacks have proven to be so influential to White folk, slang is becoming the cultural norm. Today slang usage is creeping into mainstream society. Tomorrow Black demeanor will be the cultural norm. It's already taking place in middle America. You can hear the dynamic changes in sound and music sung in popular culture. Take music by Charlie Puth for example. His hit song, Attention, has the soulful sound of Rhythm and Blues (R&B) playing throughout its entirety.

But if we are going to keep a chronology on the dynamic changes in American pop music, we must consider Michael Bolton and his hit song How Am I Suppose To Live Without You, written by Doug James and Michael Bolton in 1982. Then there's Rick Astley's Never Gonna Give You Up. Astley was, perhaps, the first White singer since Elvis Presley who captivated the hearts and minds of mainstream America with his soulful voice and R&B sound. And let us not forget Mariah Carey's debut hit single Vision of Love. Mariah stole the hearts of millions. Even after she openly identified herself as a Black (biracial) American, Mariah inspired countless millions of idolizing teen girls to sing like her. She won the hearts and souls of young White people worldwide and in a way never before witnessed. Today, countless millions of young impressionable teenage girls emulate Mariah's soulful sound through the enchantment of her music.

It appears to be inevitable! Black people are influencing popular culture in associative and in normative ways. But, how long does it take before social deviancy develops into normal behavior? How long can a people be oppressed before they learn to deviate (adapt) from their oppression? The answer to these questions may very well depend on how well Whites learn to consider Blacks and other nonwhites in the near future.

What We Can Do About It

What we can do to create a proper balance in America is, again, change the thinking strategies of dominant society. The goal is to educate and inform White people about the benefits of creating cultural opportunities. Such ambitions address the problem of what it means to be marginal in a racist, White dominated society. How do Black people adapt to life in a society that hates their very existence? How can they focus on succeeding when White people are offended over the very nature of Black people?

The daily hassles or challenges Black people confront in America has to be addressed! If, by chance, there is to be any cohesion that unifies the American people, there will have to be change in White thinking strategies.

White people tend to demonize and demoralize Blacks. The loss of confidence or hope creates a social vacuum that pulls in Black public figures who are socially resistant or narrowminded in their visions, race-based public analysis, and sensationalist practices intended to provoke excitement at the expense of public interest, into even narrower belief systems. White people lead nonwhites into relative failure by not thinking enough about how their actions will affect public interest. This type of behavior is not only characteristic of narrowminded thinking, it is associated with desperation. So, it's problematic.

It also shows how conservative Black people are when it comes down to the pressures of accepting social change. In this regard, the call to unite a nation in common purpose contributes to sociocultural problems Blacks were initially trying to overcome.

Change is coming to America, like it or not. It can come in the progressive form of assimilation or integration. Or, it can come in a higher form of a degenerate civilization. I suppose a healthy start would come from having an open dialogue at a national forum, public convention or, even, a Congressional meeting. The continuation of conflicting aims and goals of Black Nationalists and White supremacist ideals and practices mean America has taken a turn for the worse. But there is hope. A new generation of women have made their debut in Washington, DC. They are joining the Congressional halls of Congress as Congresswomen; and, they're making a difference in the world: Ayanna Pressley, D-Mass., Alexandria Ocasio-Cortez, D-NY.; Ilhan Omar, D-Minn.; and Rashida Tlaib, D-Mich. are United States Representatives. Also known as "the Squad," they are forces to reckon with.

In this chapter, we became deeply absorbed in various expressions that caused thought-provoking concerns for White people. In the next chapter, we will learn how women are making a difference in world affairs and have a great deal of adaptiveness to combat political conservatism. We will explore the way they influence our progression next in chapter 5.

Chapter 5
Making a Difference

A Manner of Expression

> You may shoot me with your words
> You may cut me with your eyes
> You may kill me with your hatefulness
> But still, like air, I'll rise.

Maya Angelou (1928 – 2014)

Black women are destined to succeed. It's true! In the poem, Still I Rise, esteemed author Maya Angelou speaks to the truth of Black women who are oppressed or treated badly by people in power. Yet, we learn after reading the poem, no one can tame the power, energy, and joy of the female spirit. Qualities like courage, fortitude, and determination enable them to rise to success in ways no man can put forth. In fact, they are doing it without the assistance needed to ensure their success. And that's against all odds.

Today, women are making a difference in the world! Black women are the most educated identity group in American society with other nonwhite women joining the ranks as intellectuals. And now that many are becoming public figures, it's only a matter of time before they emerge as national leaders. Is this new age in American history the era for nonwhite women? Will they take the helm and rebuild a greater, stronger nation, one in which nonwhites can live out productive lives without fear of social exclusion and persecution?

As the problem of competent leadership continues to haunt the nation's Capital, a new threat emerges. It appears that in order for a competent nonwhite woman to qualify as a national leader, they must have a White spouse. With the exception of Ayanna Pressley, D-Mass., every member of "the Squad" (United States Representatives Alexandria Ocasio-Cortez, D-N.Y.; Ilhan Omar, D-Minn.; and Rashida Tlaib, D-Mich.) has a White spouse. United States Supreme Court Justice Ketanji Onyika Brown Jackson also has a White spouse. Coincidence? Should it really matter? Inquiring minds think so!

We already witnessed the contradictory beliefs of Supreme Court Justice Clarence Thomas who, by the way, is married to Virginia "Ginni" Thomas, a White woman. The widespread shenanigans of Ginni were, in part, responsible for the January 6, 2021 coup attempt on the nation's Capital, an event that destabilized the lives of many Americans. And, by the way, Justice Thomas is Black! Can you understand the contradiction? Can you see a behavioral pattern forming?

The question is who are these highly qualified and competent women ultimately loyal to? Are they loyal to the American public who put them in office? Or, will they ultimately prove loyal to their spouses, White men who have no obligation to uphold the integrity or moral decency of nonwhites anywhere in the world. The potentiality of these extraordinary questions is exponential. The problem is we have no security in this generation of nonwhite women.

For the most part, these public servants have kept their spouses and mixed-race families out of the limelight, promoting business and politics first. They believe no explanation is needed. That their position in politics will speak for them and the message they hope it will send to the public. A few of their spouses said they have no need to be in the national spotlight. So, make no qualms about it. They're not hiding their relationships. And that's a problem for some people.

Some people feel like it's no coincidence that many of the younger generation of nonwhite public servants or those holding public office have White spouses. The marriage pattern is at best predictable. In fact, in the case of the 2021 Supreme Court Justice nominees, all of the so-called viable candidates had White spouses. So, the question remains, is it a requirement for nonwhite women in such high positions of power to have a White spouse?

As a tradition, women have historically supported their husbands in their endeavors. Farming, medicine, academics, whatever the case may be, the classic American woman has always stood beside her husband, even when the husband was married to his work. Now that equality of opportunity prevails for nonwhite woman, many of them are no longer homemakers but bread-winners. So, the question remains: Are these women loyal to their spouses or to the people who put them in office? The best example is a fictious account.

In the second installment of Black Panther, a Marvel Comics movie, W'Kabi, the head of security for Wakanda's Border Tribe betrayed his people. Okoye, his wife and General of the Dora Milaje, is caught in a dilemma offering two possibilities, neither of which is preferable. W'kabi asks Okaye will she fight against the love of her life (who betrayed Wakanda). Or, will she stand down in forgiveness and accept defeat. Without hesitance, Okoye says to her husband, "Wakanda forever." And with unquestionable loyalty, she quickly defeats her husband. Remember, this movie was fictious. In real world accounts, even American novelist, short story writer, poet, and social activist Alice Walker had profound loyalty to her husband. They were in an interracial marriage; and yes, he was White.

Judge Ketanji Brown Jackson certainly was appointed a Supreme Court seat even after being publicly humiliated by Republican representatives in a Senate Committee Judicial Hearing. Today, Justice Jackson serves as an associate justice of the United States Supreme Court. Might her marital status have anything to do with her appointment? Perhaps, it was political? Whatever the case may be, this potential problem continues to aggravate the crises of potentially competent leadership in American society. Thus, threats of a degenerate form of higher civilization remains but, potentially, at the expense of American citizens.

Many people have given up on the land of the free and the home of the brave. They say that the feeling of love, devotion, and sense of attachment to America and its bureaucracy has gone. The reason behind it is the political process is corrupt and immoral. That there is no political party worthy of their consideration. For them, there is no need to vote. As the American public learns more about its true history, more-and-more people are rejecting the idea of American patriotism. Political corruption has created awareness among many Americans. They have no choice. They cannot unlearn the truth, the truth being America's vicious legacies of racism and White supremacy. And while conservatism appears to be tapering off, right-winged extremism is increasing in popularity.

The Rise of Modern Extremism

White Nationalists, extremists or, as we will call them, the far-right consists primarily of White supremacist and antigovernment fanatics who hold extreme political and, sometimes, fanatical religious views. Although, there are a few extremist groups that focus their energies on resolving problems like abortion and immigration.

Today, more than one hundred right-wing extremists are campaigning for political office. I caution these candidates have the potential to sway public opinion away from what is considered ordinary or acceptable discourse. Instead, they learned to shift topics to extreme political and religious ideology. While a few candidates lost their campaign races, results from the presidential primary elections demonstrate that having ties to right-wing extremist groups is no longer a political problem.

In fact, of the one hundred nineteen right-wing extremists participating in the US primaries, approximately one quarter of the total candidates won their election, placing them much closer to winning the general elections and gaining access to political power. In fact, of the actual thirty political candidates who won their campaigns, ten won by a narrow margin of less than twelve percent.

The far-right subscribes to a range of fanatical political and religious ideology, especially the ones who espouse antigovernment extremism like, the Oath Keepers, a militia movement that recruits former military personnel, White supremacists, and antisemitic groups. What's even more disturbing is other candidates actively seek to undermine the United States electoral process by promoting White supremacist propaganda, creating election conspiracies, and by participating in the January 6, 2021 terrorist attack on the nation's Capital.

With the younger generation of women public servants now at-risk for the violence associated with far-right extremism, the question is how far will they lag behind in resolving this new and greater threat to national security? Will they place women's issues on hold? Or, is this level of national security a woman's issue? Only time will tell. But, how much time will it take? Or, will their efforts prove to be too little, too late?

What We Can Do About It

What we can do to instigate change in thinking strategies is critical yet identical to America's current state of progression. We are living in the age of racial consciousness. America is struggling to find her true identity. The solution is simple. Yet, its potential challenges are twofold: The first resolution has yet to be eradicated due to a certain blindness to structural and institutional defects in public and political practices.

The reason for the cultural divide widening among the American people is due to the lack of political follow-through from both Democratic and Republican Parties. For me, the first example that comes to mind is the problem people have with singing or standing for the National Anthem.

Colin Kaepernick first alerted the American public to the problem of singing or standing for the National Anthem. What a brilliant sacrifice Colin Kaepernick made as he lost his sports career for kneeling during the patriotic ceremony. For years, the problem Blacks had was in getting the media to follow through on the topic. Kaepernick got the controversial anthem widespread attention. On the other hand, his actions infuriated many nations in the West. Both political parties, being short-sighted, debated the problem at-hand.

Today, standing for the National Anthem incites controversy. The resolution to the problem is, yet again, simple: It's not the first half of the Anthem that is controversial but the second half. Since not many people even know the second half of the National Anthem (because it's racist), then it needs to be rewritten. And, it can be that simple. Just rewrite the second half of the National Anthem: problem resolved!

The second challenge is potentially personal yet has grounds to be a matter of national priority. On the one hand, we have what appears to be competent nonwhite women joining the nation's ranks as politicians and public servants. Specifically, this new generation of sophomoric class Congresswomen are challenging every aspect of the White establishment in Washington, DC. They show great awareness and concern for nonwhite issues. They formed a progressive multiracial coalition as a major response to political conservatism. Such actions include, but are not limited to, holding conservatives in the Republican Party accountable for preserving their self-serving values. Progressive actions also work in response to political conservatism in the Democratic Party.

For the first time in American politics, conservatives are being called out for their fear of change. The push for change has people who thought they were progressive stepping down from central leadership roles. Nancy Pelosi recently announced she was stepping down from her role as House Democratic Leader to make room for a new generation of leadership.

For the first time in American history, political conservatism is being confronted and surmounted. The progressive potential of this new generation of Congressional women and their need to hold political conservatives accountable for their political values is not only courageous but brilliant. They are instigating social change in American politics by creating public awareness at the grass-roots level and at the expense of political conservativism.

Unfortunately, this style of politics, the entire ideology of progressive politics, is being threatened by conservatives in both political parties. Many of today's women leaders are being accosted. They are under the constant threat of violence by people who are averse to change. If no one figures out how to change their thinking strategies, conservatives and their conservative supporters will continue to uphold conservatism as a wholesome part of the American value system. This potential threat continues to create a social vacuum filled by boldly defiant White Nationalists or the far-right who strongly identify with their own race and vigorously support their self-interests. If progressives do not properly follow through, extremists and their conservative supporters could set the country back, exhausting its progressive potential. Yet, this new generation of progressive women in politics have only begun to show the true potential of progressive leadership.

On the other hand, these women are under the potential threat of social compromise. Many of the new Congresswomen (and public servants) serving today, and those making power moves in American politics, are threatened by the potential compromise of interracial marriage. And that's the second potential challenge for progressive women in politics.

You heard right, quite a few nonwhite public servants are married to White men who have a natural allegiance to people considered to be characteristic members of the White establishment. Although they may yet not show allegiance to extremists and conservatives, who's to say that under the threat of social compromise, such as the problem Whites now face with White genetic annihilation, they will not develop a relaxed or informal attitude toward nonwhites. Like many married couples in American society, few spouses can sidestep the potential problem of breaking faith or the promise of commitment and loyalty to their significant others who may align themselves with the White establishment just to preserve racial integrity.

In this way, the relative failure of political conservatism created an opportunity for young, talented, and defiant political integrationists and progressive women politicians. Many of these women are bold and share daring visions, are able to conduct multiracial analyses, and show an ability to take risks in politics that, quite frankly, challenges the status quo of political conservatism in American society.

They boldly and defiantly protest leaders who have narrow visions and sensationalist practices that show the xenophobic nature of political conservatism. This type of progressive practice, the integrationist approach to American politics is quite characteristic of social inclusion from a society more and more accepting of social change. It is also characteristic of a country that is desperate to shed its ugly xenophobic practices and belief systems. Indeed, America is changing its social path.

Change is indeed coming to America. The question is will it be enough to reverse the plight of its invisible people to include its most vulnerable. The answer to that question is yes; it can be more than enough to remedy the wretched problem of poverty, homelessness, and marginalization in American society but only if we continue to candidly confront its existence. It has nothing to do with the return of a Messiah, loyal Christian worship, finding a new approach to community organizing, a new organization emerging, or receiving financial support from a collection of caring nations.

No, it involves working through the lived experiences of a potentially dangerous people. These people, right-wing political extremists, who created political conservatism to permanently undermine the critical consciousness and moral commitment needed to take Democratic accountability, did so through sustained public visibility. It also downplays the crucial crisis not only in political leadership but in American society. Just remember, America's political system is not broken. It is designed to do just what it does: oppress our most vulnerable. Our job is to dismantle it. Then we can rebuild the structural and institutional processes that make it possible to give a voice to our disadvantaged and reverse the plight of our most vulnerable: Black Americans.

In this chapter, we've seen that women are making a difference not only in American government, but also in American society. They are gaining a great deal of respect from America as a whole. But, we've also seen how violence factors in as women earn their place in today's society. In this next chapter, we will turn our attention to which expressions help and are helping Black people to adapt and overcome in American society.

A Manner of Expression

Chapter 6
Negro Spirituals
and its Contributions to Black Music

A Manner of Expression

> Knowledge makes a man unfit to be a slave.
> Frederick Douglass (1818 – 1895)

In his autobiography, Narrative of the Life of Frederick Douglass: An American Slave, Frederick Douglass explores the power of literacy in slavery. In his quest to read and write, he quickly developed disdain for his position as a slave. But, his greatest lesson was in learning that the slave master greatly feared suffering the same exclusionary methods of subjugation they imposed on Black people throughout their intellectual history.

After the Civil War (1865), some Whites believe their past misdeeds would lead to some ironic moment in history. But, the majority of White slave holders became bitter and undignified over the loss of their ability to produce free slave labor. Racism resulted from the notion of having been treated unfairly for loss of property. Simply said, racism exists because dominant White society lost certain entitlements and privileges they had during antebellum.

Before The War

Southern economies were thriving due to slavery. Whites were starving in the Northern states due to the scarcity of jobs and lack of available resources caused by free slave labor predominating in the South. Although the South was unabashed by the suffering of White people in

Northern states, the government sought to end chattel slavery thus ending the financial reign of Whites in the South. This event is what caused the Civil War (1861 – 1865).

A Brief Consideration of
The Enslavement Process

They say communication is the first line of defense. To win battles against any war, you must first establish communications or cut off the enemy's communications. Europeans work diligently, for centuries even, just to destroy the African communication system. In fact, Europeans knew if they could not stop Africans from communicating with one another, then there would be no slavery.

Europeans redirected communications by pitting Africans against one another, which gave them the leverage needed to justify the enslavement of certain African groups. For the enslaved, Whites destroyed many opened forms of African communication. The slave master put an end to the existence of African language, culture, and other traditional African systems used to identify or establish open forms of communications. Why? If Africans could not communicate to one another then, quite simply, they could not revolt against the very people who enslaved them, at least, not in large masses. As well, the slave master moved Africans around, frequently, from plantation-to-plantation.

Not only were slaves moved around, frequently, African children were forcibly removed from their environment and reared on other plantations, miles apart from their biological parents. You asked, "Why?" Well, that's a good question! African children were reared in different environments just to prevent them from learning their heritage, establishing communications with Africans from similar regions, and to prevent them from learning how to revote against White people and the tyranny of racial oppression.

As Famed Negro-breaker Willie Lynch once said:

> "…keep the slave but take the mind so that the slave remains physically strong but psychologically weak and dependent on the slave master for survival."

Frederick Douglass spoke on his dependency of the slave master before learning how to read and write. Dependency was merely one of their methods used to control slaves. The slave master was diabolical in his methods of slavery.

The slave master established breeding plantations usually on the indigenous islands in the Caribbean also known as the Americas or the American islands. Slaves were left under some of the most horrific breeding conditions imaginable. Have you ever heard of the term "motherfucker?" Well, the slave master use to place a bag over the heads of male slaves to prevent them from seeing who they were having sex with. In many cases, the male slave was forced to engage in sexual relations with close relatives like aunts, cousins, sisters, daughters, even their own mothers which, apparently, was common, hence the derogatory term "motherfucker." If ever you see an albino male or female, understand it develops from having close ordered pair-bonds, otherwise inbreeding. Young male children were also taught to engage in homosexual activities at the master's discretion.

Oh, I tell you, the slave master was truly diabolical in his wickedness and perversion. An important tactic of Negro-breaking, today, buck-breaking or butt-busting, was to take a recalcitrant male slave and then rape him in front of the slave colonists. Then he, because most slave masters were men, would have slave-hands beat any recalcitrant slave to within an inch of living and in front of remaining nigger males, females, and nigger children just to imprint the memories into their conscious minds.

The sexual abuse and, sometimes, murder of a recalcitrant slave or any slave having a stubbornly resistant attitude toward slavery or the slave master occurred so other slaves would not be resistant to future breading with family, friends, strangers, or others. Also, beatings took place to prevent slaves from resisting the slave master's unwanted sexual advances toward the remaining nigger males, females, and nigger children. Obviously, the slave master was right down sick, twisted, and psychosadistic in his wickedness and perversion. Yet, through it all, the slave remained resilient. Through their resilience, adaptiveness, and responsiveness, over time, slaves managed to pave their way to freedom. How so, you ask?

Slave Songs of the United States

Slave songs of the United States, otherwise slave hymns or Negro Spirituals, were used to open lines of communication between the doors of slavery and the road to freedom for many slaves. Negro spirituals (as I like to call them) were not only spiritually uplifting songs that told inspiring stories that motivated slaves to work throughout long agonizing days in the field, but code-talking that communicated calls or roadmaps to freedom.

Spirituals were communicated by slaves and through the use of spoken word hymns. In each of these hymns were messages that often directed a slave to safehouses. There, at secret or safe locations, a slave could hide safely until he or she was eventually picked up by a person or people opposed to the practice of slavery. Abolitionists would see to the slave's safety until he, she, or they could be transported to free societies somewhere largely in North America.

Negro spirituals like Wade in the Water was sung to inform a potential runaway slave that the best way to lose the bloodhounds, dogs sent by the slave master, was to walk long distances through the water to prevent them from tracking the runaway. The coded language in the song that bespoke an important message to the slave was, "God's Gonna Trouble the Water."

Origins of the Negro spiritual, quite possibly, began in the church. The church was a safe haven for slaves. What do I mean? Well, the church served as a sanctuary of refuge or safety for slaves. It was one of the only places where a slave could rest, learn, and worship. The slave master figured out religious worship was one of the best practices for a slave to learn obedience, the church believing in corporal punishment at the time.

The church has always been used by slaves as a source of refuge. Many began to congregate and communicate with the church congregation and among themselves. As an institution, its rich history has long since been established in Black culture. Rooted in the slave experience, the church became an immediate substitution for African worship because of its ability to satisfy their emotional or spiritual needs in ways village-based worship and social practices use to long before Black people left Africa. Today, the Black church has become the main source or an important factor in their efforts to cope with stress and oppression, especially placing religious values ahead of everything else.

The church became a hallmark or the main element of the Black experience. Even after chattel slavery, newly freed slaves were said to have a profound need for religious revival. The church served to improve the mental condition or strengthen the conscious minds of Black folk. Newly freed Negros or Blacks living in segregated environments revealed a few important survival strategies used by the church to cope with the overwhelming impact of stress and oppression.

Religious worship or prayer and singing left many slaves with a feeling of reverence and adoration toward a God. Also, they believed that religious worship and Negro spirituals helped them to establish a fundamental belief or a basic way of living that connected them to a God. It gave many the strength and courage to establish belief in one all-powerful being who would correct man's indiscretions toward humanity. Religious worship helped them develop certain characteristics in common, important adaptations and coping skills needed to unify the integrity of Black folk. As a result, they built their own communities and social structures.

Churches, kin systems, and family associations were often developed in the Black community to help buffer the impact of slavery and the psychological stress of coping with segregation after slavery. In this way, Blacks began to value church as a mutual support system. The church also helped to improve social awareness for many freed Black people. So, it quickly gained in appreciation for its ability to develop the family unit as a source of strength.

Over the years, the church helped Black people to establish prominence. Not only was the church responsible for helping Blacks establish prominence, it helped them establish a presence and voice. Now that many Blacks were becoming educators, public speakers, carpenters, artisans and architects, lawyers, doctors, and other prominent pillars of the community, even Black mayors began to surface in America and as part of a wholesome American value system, they began to experience strong and adverse reactions from their oppressors.

Blacks established their own cities and towns as well. So, they began to stand out as a viable threat to dominant White society. The malicious intentions of dominant society quickly became evident through the use of state-sponsored terrorism. It was introduced in the form of public lynchings, Black codes, White supremacy during reconstruction, eugenics, and other unlawful use of violence and intimidation, especially in the pursuit of happiness and their political fight against home grown terrorism.

At every level of consideration, when there was supposed to be peace, Black people found themselves under attack for political, economic, and religious reasons. There was an eleven-year campaign of hate waged against Blacks during the Reconstruction Period. Then during the 1890's, as Black folk came into prominence, dominant society saw fit to destroy entire towns built by Blacks. Several towns and communities were turned into lakes. That's right! While many residents continued to reside in their homes, entire towns were submerged under tons of water. Others had their lands stolen only to be offered a plaque as reparations. The University of Alabama is one such example. Yet, Black folk continue to show remark-able resilience, adaptiveness, and responsiveness in the presence of overwhelming stress and oppression.

Fast-forward to today and we're well into the new millennium. Yet, the vicious legacy of racism and White supremacy continues. Although Blacks have learned to negotiate with dominant White society, they continue to face strong and adverse reactions by their White counterparts. Still, there is no public backlash against racism in America or against any Western nations today. Thus, with all of the impressive negotiation skills, oral and written, Black people continue to be exploited, oppressed, and humiliated by existing powers of authority.

Black people are the most vocal or outspoken identity group in American society. But, they have yet to obtain or bring about racial equality and social justice through protest and open discourse. Dr. Martin Luther King, Jr. once organized the Poor Man's Campaign to free Black people from economic oppression. With all of the protesting and marching demonstrations disturbing and intimidating the masses during the civil rights movement, it was the Poor Man's Campaign that led to his assassination. Perhaps, Blacks need to consider revisiting his goal of establishing racial equity for the people rather than racial equality.

As the first line of defense, Blacks continuously communicated their cries for equality through music. If it wasn't through gospel music, it was rhythm and blues (R&B). In a previous chapter, we mentioned Billy Holiday and her controversial song, Strange Fruit. I believe most Black music is communicated through coded language due to their oppression.

Up until this point, we discussed the powerful role of Negro spirituals and how it was weaponized as the basis for disseminating important information to the oppressed as a first line of defense against oppression. I gave examples of this action at the beginning of this chapter. Next, we will discuss how Blacks took important messages from the church to the open streets.

From Church to the Open Streets

If you haven't figured it out yet, Negro Spirituals gained its start from the Church. To find out what you missed, turn back to the beginning of this chapter.

While Negro spirituals may have its origins in the church, it was made for the streets, the people. Negro spirituals were created using broken English. Slang, Black vernacular, and Ebonics made up the language used to communicate trouble, hardship or sorrow, or the covert possibility of freedom for the enslaved. Over the years, and throughout the centuries, the style of songs changed but the message it communicates remain the same.

The Blues, Rhythm and Blues, and now Hip-Hop, street rhymes, or rap music are the latest genres derived from Negro spirituals. That's right! I did not studder. These music styles communicate some of the most important political messages the world ever witnessed. From the 1860's and early 1960's, the Blues incorporated spirituals, work songs, field hollers, shouts, chants as well as poetry and rhymes from simple narratives as told by the Black American experience. It later made way for Rhythm and Blues.

Rhythm and Blues or, simply, R&B was born out of the Blues in the 1940's. The lyrics in R&B often incorporated the Black experience of pain and joy, their quest for freedom or liberty, along with social and political movements that led to triumphs and failures in personal relationships, economics both personal and political, and aspirations. Although, the yawning gulf between aspiration and reality created greater cynicism among its many skeptics.

Rap music, which is a part of Hip-Hop culture, is a music genre originating in New York City during the 1970's. Its early origins are rooted in Negro spirituals, country music, grassroots, jazz, R&B, and much more, all of which originated from Black folk. Its stylized rhythm commonly accompanies rhymes or poetic language, spoken not sung, and in a chant.

Now what's unusual about this style of music is its ability to ignite a crowd or start a movement. The music, itself, groomed entire communities. Not only did rap music prepare entire communities to fight against "the powers that be," it awakened a great nation to its ugly xenophobic resentment. First, it communicated significant points that were of political, social, and moral importance to the powers that be or the existing powers of authority.

Through rap music, Blacks began a campaign to communicate highly political messages about the social injustices and inhumane conditions existing in Black communities. The Message, written by Grand-Master Flash, was one of the first pieces of rap music that mainstreamed across America. "Don't touch me cause I'm close to the edge" were the lyrics he used as the hook in the famous rap song. It communicated a coded message that warned people about the realities of street life, pleading for positive change in an environment disadvantaged by mainstream society.

The Message, first released in 1982, was the first rap song to find its way into the homes of affluent White Americans. It influenced the opinions and mindset of countless White children from the younger generation. The rap song was among the first to change the social dynamics of American culture. The second song that influenced American culture was The Breaks, written earlier, in 1980, by Kurtis Blow.

No longer were White children listening to opera and classical music. Even Rock n' Roll took a back seat to rap music as this cultural juggernaut quickly overwhelmed the cultural mainstream. The style of dress changed considerably for White children, and street dances emerged only to become part of a new dance craze for mainstream culture. Ironically, more-and-more Whites from the younger generation gravitated toward racial integration. America also began to experience population shifts in demographics.

Over time, Whites became more accepting of Blacks than in previous years. The vast majority of Whites now support Blacks and their rights to public office, access to public accommodations, fair housing, and so forth. Yet, the violence created by Whites toward Blacks continues to spark conflict and hatred between them. Unfortunately, at every point in history, where Whites have opened the lines of communication between themselves and Blacks, there were factions that dissent from an increasing majority.

There are many forms of communications. Oral and written are just two of the main forms effectively used to recognize or acknowledge social problems. Other forms of communication involve bodily expressions or gestures. Forms like open protests and marching demonstrations alert the world to positive or negative events occurring within the context of human society. The goal is to make an emotional appeal to bring peace of mind usually to a dire situation.

Music is, perhaps, the best way to communicate messages to the masses. Why? It has the ability to influence us in good or bad ways. If you're a church goer, think about the gospels you sing during church services. What feelings do you experience? If you're a dancer, think about the grove that gets you into the mood to dance. We associate pleasant and often important feelings with music even though it may not provide us information that will change our situation.

In the last half of this chapter, we discussed how Negro spirituals morphed from church hymns to street music in American society. Although its sound changes over the years, the basis and the message communicated remain the same. Hip-Hop or classic rap music provides historical contexts for the way in which Whites and Blacks perceive one another. In addition, the amount of education or information the message communicates has important determinants in the progress made between identity groups.

What We Can Do About It

The nature of relationships that exist between or among separate and distinct cultural systems presents itself in three fundamental ways. First, it's a matter of displaced aggression or antiblack racism. The amount of antiblack racism gives way to the notion that White people enjoy greater privileges and opportunities than nonwhites solely on the basis of skin color. That regardless of their accomplishments and acclaims, in American society, Black people will always assume social roles ordinarily performed by people less able, and solely on the basis of their skin color.

Second, antiblack racism is based on excessive expectations nonwhite groups have about both Whites and Blacks. This perception holds Whites to excessively high standards different from that believed to be true of Blacks. The double standards in cultural expectations assume Whites and Blacks are natural enemies and thus compete against each other as a means of survival. So, when Blacks complain about poor living conditions or their economic disadvantages, other nonwhite identity groups believe Black people are naturally incompetent and unable to socially compete in a high-tech modern society. As a result, more-and-more Blacks become vulnerable as nonwhite groups refuse to hire them based solely on cultural stereotypes.

Although Whites claim to be inherently com-passionate people and portray themselves as the saviors of humanity, beliefs in that false narrative strongly resonates among nonwhite groups more so than what is actually true. The notion that White people have historically victimized Blacks in order to control a narrative that whitewashes an important history and legacy of greatness accomplished by a downtrodden people is simply unfitting to believe by the majority of nonwhites, many of whom are looking to capitalize off of cheap and menial labor.

In this way, many Blacks are forced to take on duties and responsibilities that present the false impression they are inherently weak and, by nature, less able to function alongside Whites. This false belief reinforces poor perception among other nonwhite groups. In turn, many of these groups believe that the cultural stereotypes about Blacks are, in fact, true. The result is the continuous denial of a history and tragedy endured by Blacks.

More importantly, having a poor perception of Black people means they will forever be saddled with certain social stigmas, stigmas that will never escape them. Yet, as Black people are considered to be the most loyal and patriotic identity group in the entire world, they are charged with the moral crime of betraying the very people said to have sacrificed themselves to help them. For those reasons, Black people are destined to become a permanent underclass not only in American society but among world cultures.

Third, antiblack racism as displaced aggression shows the amount of resentment White people have toward Blacks and their potentiality. Such indignation suggest that Whites are bitter toward Blacks. Whites fear that Blacks will never overcome their current situation. So, if left up to fate, Blacks will create a degenerate form of higher civilization. Who they are, where they come from, and their ability to achieve at life is inconsequential to the pain and suffering they endure from White people.

I have no idea why other nonwhite identity groups, like Africans, Asians, and others, compete against Black Americans to the end point of bitter resentment. They receive assistance from a government that makes it possible for them to succeed at life despite past indiscretions with the powers that be. The emotional mixture of disappointment, disgust, anger and, seemingly, large amounts of bitter envy among remaining nonwhites appears to be elicited in the presence of insult and injury. But, at a time when nonwhites are exposed to racism and xenophobia, they should view Black people as a source of strength rather than an obstacle in the fight for social justice.

Now, to better relations for Black people in America, there needs to be open communication among identity groups so there is a sufficient exchange of information and news, especially about recent or important events in politics, the economy, various communities, and social settings. The importance of staying informed on current events is so people can learn what resources can or should be distributed in terms of racial equity and equality.

Also, the government needs to assist the oppressed to better establish an independent economy. Economies are the building blocks of communities. Without an independent economy, communities cannot prosper. So, there can only be behavior that exists contrary to law. What I mean is an economy stabilizes a community so its residents can succeed at citizenry, forging close and like-minded personal relationships with existing residents, building and showing empathy toward each other, and learning how to communicate through common interest.

In this regard, there needs to be some redistribution of wealth and power to prevent the lack of fairness or justice that exists for oppressed people continuously treated poorly by existing powers of authority. Without sustainable or preventative measures placed in American society, there can be no communities or sense of sharing, safety, or belonging that communities can provide. In a sense, cooperation should exist to make the situation fair or better for everyone.

In this chapter, I covered a few important points on how Blacks communicate their intentions under oppressive conditions. In the resolution section, I talked about how we can better intergroup relations for Black people. In the next chapter, we will turn our attention to how necessity created the means to survive. The mother of inventions awaits you in chapter 7.

Chapter 7
The Mother of Invention

Necessity is the mother of invention.

Plato (427 BCE - 348 BCE)

Plato once said, "Necessity is the mother of invention." When you develop a need for something, it becomes imperative to find ways to acquire it. That's proverb! We all desire to acquire things; and, we live in a world where we work to acquire them.

Think about the reason why you work. You work in order to acquire money. Money allows you to purchase all sorts of things: cars, toys, fancy houses, et cetera. Now, think about the things you buy, things that are necessities: food, clothing, and shelter. The more necessary the item, the greater the increase in demand. Thus, it becomes harder to keep a ready source in supply. We call this scenario the law of supply and demand.

Blacks were in high demand as free and, eventually, cheap labor. From zero dark thirty to can't see at night slaves, well most of them, were used to pick cotton, farm, and clear fields. Those who were taught skilled labor eventually supplied the means to complete the labor efficiently. This is the reason why so many researchers believe and have basic proof that Eli Whitney did not invent the cotton gin, which I vaguely mention again later in this chapter. How did the slave meet the demands of the slave master? How did the slave overcome their situation? And, more importantly, what does this chapter have to do with the rest of this book? I will attempt to answer these and other questions shortly.

Coming into Their Own

So far, we've been talking about why contemporary Black expressions offend White people. Well, this chapter is no different. The fact that Black people became fully self-efficient after slavery despite the maltreatment of their people was all the more reason for White people to find them so offensive. The development of inventions served as greater proof that Blacks were adapting to their situation. In fact, they were coming into their own. In other words, they were beginning to show greater manners of expression than Whites. And, that is more than enough to cause resentment from Whites.

After slavery, Black people became profoundly resourceful out of necessity. During the period of US Reconstruction (1866 – 1877), they began to establish their own towns and community resources. Churches, community town halls, and kin systems, they even had their own militias, just to give you an idea of how developed their resources were. In many cases, Blacks were recognized as some of the most successful and influential professionals in the business world. All of this out of a growing need to survive.

What is crucial is that the various ways Black people express themselves developed as a means of survival. The learning of art, music, and education were all taught as part of a greater need to survive. Even during slavery, there were various ways to acquire trades and skillsets.

It was necessary to teach or train some slaves. But after the Civil War (1865), other slaves taught themselves. Black-smith, carpenter, even architect and mason were among the many skillsets self-taught. You see, the goal of American slavery was to get rich or maintain an affluent lifestyle without engaging in physical labor. So, many of the slaves, former and current, were already skilled laborers. That's right! Not everyone picked cotton.

We may not know as much as once thought. But what we do know is that after the Civil War, Black inventors like Granville Tailer Woods emerged across America. Granville was the first Black American mechanical and electrical engineer to be recognized as an inventor. He held more than fifty patents in the United States. Granville, who was self-taught, dedicated most of his career to developing trains and streetcars.

Blacks have had, as a necessity, the need to survive ever since their arrival on the great shores of America. Since then, Black people have been in dire need to reduce the amount of stress associated with working under extreme conditions. Just remember, US slavery was the name of the trade industry. Picking cotton was the national game, well at least it was for most.

Africans were stolen from their homeland and brought here to America as slave labor. They would endure name changes too! From African to Negro to colored person, and then from colored person to Afro-American to person of color from which most Blacks felt comfortable. And now, many Blacks believe the term African American is a politically correct statement. Although, more Blacks from the younger generation feel a warm and inviting connection to the term Black American, just to bring the masses to comfort.

So, when the need for cheap labor became imperative, Whites found ways to acquire Blacks. Blacks, on the other hand, were forced to find out ways of reducing slave labor for themselves. For example, the advent of the thermostat/temperature control, the modern toilet, the automatic elevator doors, and improvements on other technologies such as the telegraph, telephone, phonograph, and the safety circuit, Blacks like Granville T. Woods invented that which was in high demand or necessary. Hence, necessity is the mother of invention.

People like Lewis H. Latimer were the originators of numerous inventions because of a necessity to supply a need that was in high demand. Besides, creating inventions reduced the number of work-related stress laborers were forced to endure. Call it the advent of Black ingenuity. Make no mistake about it, when Black people learned to express themselves by way of innovations and inventions, it even put money in the pockets of White people like American inventor and businessman Thomas A. Edison.

Thomas Edison, as he is known throughout the world, owned a business firm where he hired a team of draftsmen to design various inventions. To my surprise, after the draftsmen completed the task at-hand, Edison would tell a team of trusted inventors to change the schematics around so they could patent it in his name. Thomas Edison would go on to patent over one thousand inventions in this way.

Most Black inventers were not allowed to patent inventions or trademark professional names and logos. Perhaps, it was a win for both parties as some Whites would give credit to Blacks through diaries, log books and, in a few cases, by testimony. Black people are the creators of more inventions than most of us will ever know.

A Brief History of Black Inventors

It was usually out of necessity for survival many Blacks learn to accommodate the scheme of White production. This meant there would be countless Black inventors who would shape American history. However, the notion of Black inventions did not originate in the Americas. No, it originated in Africa.

One of the main reasons why Blacks were stolen from the continent was due to their knowledge of science and architecture. The problem was European governments failed to disclosed the truth about who were being enslaved.

It is said most inventions were the innovative projects and solutions of ancient Egyptians or Kamites. Although many inventions are considered innovations of Egypt, most were created by Africans beyond Egyptian boundaries. Even before Egyptologists lightened up the images on numerous Egyptian paintings, statues, and figurines, these images were depicted as Brown and Black people who had inherently African features that resembled people from the African diaspora.

Louder Than Words

The seventeenth-century English philosopher John Locke once argued that the best interpreter of man's thoughts was his actions. Does doing something reinforce your beliefs in what you've done? Thomas Jefferson often complained about the horrors of slavery but was a productive slave owner. One of our founding fathers and the first person to become President of the United States of America, George Washington had two Negro concubines he cherished. But he was a mean-spirited, vicious brut who had the teeth knocked out of the mouths of slaves just to fashion a pair of teeth that he could call his own.

Look at the level of consistency! Actions speak louder than words. And the White man's actions reinforce to the world his intentions. That's why it is so hard to believe that White men, all of a sudden, had a change of heart toward the very people they oppressed. It surely wasn't their job to make life easier for slaves who endured working in the fields under extremely perverse and agonizing conditions. So, for researches like myself, we find it a bit suspect that someone like Eli Whitney would go out of his way to invent the cotton gin. Or that US Presidents like Joe Biden, Bill Clinton, and the Bushes were misunderstood and had noble intentions toward Black people. In fact, we often say the only thing the White man ever invented was the US Patent and Trademark office. That way, he could steal everyone else's inventions.

Since the Civil War (1865), there has been numerous Black inventions patented and, unfortunately, under the assumed identity of the White man. While it is true that situation dictates, Black people have always tried to succeed beyond their situation. Situations trigger the creative processes. How to escape from bondage, how to avoid abuse or the systematic destruction of a people, et cetera. The whole gold of survival is how not to become a victim of your environment.

Many Black inventors were just that, victims, not necessarily of their immediate environment, but victims of their social environment. In this case, *social environment* refers to a person's racial heritage. Does anyone remember The Dred Scott Decision? A judge ruled that the Black man has no rights to which a White man was bound to respect. White inventors understood the full position of Black inventors and, often, took advantage of their situation. Countless Black inventions have been lost under the dominion of dominant White society.

Today, we find evidence of Black inventions but through diaries, recording logs, state archives, and journals, thanks to the brave people who were courageous enough to leave us hints. We also find actual proof that Black people innovated and created inventions that revolutionized modern-day America. Although much of the proof is scrutinized, there are a few cases where Blacks held victory over their White counterparts. Lewis H.

Latimer took Thomas Edison to court and won a decision against him for a few patents filed as his inventions. Latimer was an inventor and the chief draftsman for Thomas Edison. But that was just the beginning.

There would be countless battles for patent rights won and lost. Most of those battles lost would be lost forever. But the ability to invent, the creative process to think independent of the White establishment, would continue through the science of math, art, music, and other manifestations of the human intellectual achievement.

Remember, we're discussing the days of segregation. Blacks were teased apart from the cultural mainstream. Separate schools, hotels, hospitals, toilets, parks, even telephone booths and water fountains were segregated as a standard national policy. There were no White people teaching in Black schools and colleges. So, in many cases, Black people, who learned under the light of candles, were self-taught.

Interesting fact: The majority of the Historically Black Colleges and Universities (HBCU or HBCUs) originated from 1865 to 1900. Although, the greatest number of HBCUs began in 1867. The reason these historic colleges and universities were written into law was due to American segregation. The second Morrill Act of 1890 required any State to provided land-grants to establish institutions for Blacks if admission was not allowed elsewhere.

Today, we see a lot of raw potential from Black folk through the creative process of street art such as graffiti, dance, and music. That's right! Hip-Hop culture has taken the world by storm. And with that cultural juggernaut going global, contemporary Black expressions have the potential of becoming something more than what the future holds. In fact, it can become a universal norm.

A Problem of Cultural Nihilism

The problem is universal norms reinforce the idea of cultural nihilism in America. As America becomes a global entity, White people believe they are losing important grounds. Many of them believe the world no longer has meaning. More-and-more, they are feeling like victims. And it is due to racial integration or the immigration habits and migration patterns of nonwhites.

White people believe that racial diversity creates genocide. They are refusing to coexist with nonwhites in fear of white genetic annihilation. Many Whites are raised under the impression that they are the only racial group to contribute a legacy of gains to the world. Most continue to exist under the assumption that the first civilizations came from out of Europe. So, through them all things are possible. This understanding goes with the advent of technology such as the automobile. With the truth about Black inventions and other Black innovations surfacing, many White people are forced to accept the contributions Black people make to America. The idea of Black intelligence or Black people expressing themselves in productive ways is difficult for them to believe or accept.

White people have a problem in accepting the truth about Blacks. Regardless of their intellectual prowess, Black people are not supposed to be intelligent. This notion comes with the understanding that Blacks are not creative, are unimaginative, and unoriginal. Although many are happy-go-lucky, the mere idea of Negros mastering any-thing more than performance arts or social entertainment is, well, problematic for White people.

As more world cultures begin to see Blacks as okay people, many begin to form a mutual trust. They develop firm beliefs in Blacks' natural ability to function as others do. In fact, through various forms of interaction, many cultures consider Black people to be exceptional, specifically, in their ability to adapt to novel situations. Their natural ability to adapt and negotiate in a hostile environment causes further transgressions among White people.

Whites become irritated as Blacks become more successful. As Blacks learn to express themselves in greater feats, occasional incidents continue to spark conflict and hatred between Whites and Blacks. For example, a Black person is murdered at the hands of White police officers when the situation did not seem to warrant such violence. The victim is a young Black male whose only crime is walking alone to school. The more productive or successful Black people become, the more they attract violence from Whites. Posturing among Whites and over contemporary Black expressions is a way for them to place blame onto Blacks for any criminal mischief or wrongdoings. So, there is growing resistance to the success of Black people in American society.

The question is, will White people continue to move toward healthy racial attitudes? Or, will they continue to engage in activities that resist further change? For example, it does appear that Whites support racial integration more than in the past two decades. But, talk of their support may just be lip service. That is to say, today's Whites appear to hold healthy racial attitudes toward Blacks on the surface. But underneath, they may continue to harbor racial feelings. In this way, their general feelings of equality may be superficial. It's easy to support racial equality in public. But, standing by your word when it actually means something has costly implications. Whether Whites experience genuine ambivalence about Black Americans remains to be seen. Or, are they just blatantly racist toward them? Either way, Black people remain cautious.

In the early 1900's, at the turn of the 20th century, world cultures said they'd be happy to conduct business with Black Americans just not Whites. That statement and decision sparked a killing spree whereby White people massacred Blacks in various communities cross the American South. Most Blacks were driven out of their homes and communities. Other Blacks had their communities and towns submerged under tons of water. The end results were affluent White communities and beautiful lake-front swimming resorts. Today, many of these towns are forgotten, still submerged under tons of water.

As you can see, there is growing concern in the Black community about the nihilistic threat of Whites. Although Black people who rise above their circumstances can greatly benefit American society, it seems to be especially distressing to Whites who seek out social dominance. Integration may be a healthier adaptation as we already know. However, it clearly causes problems for Whites who choose not to adapt to the changing tapestry of American culture. On the other hand, cultural nihilism appears to satisfy some cultural expectation of society. Although it is one of the least healthy of cultural adaptations, it seems to be more realistic, especially as the country moves steadily toward diversity or racial integration.

What We Can Do About It

What we can do about cultural nihilism is reduce the course of action. To do so, we must confront its very existence. But first, we must understand the current state of affairs.

The situation of Blacks in America is three-fold: First, Blacks are constantly being abused and murdered by White police officers. The killings are more often endorsed by the State while federal agencies turn a blind-eye. There must be new models of intention in place and made readily available to train law enforcement as a necessary course of action. Each model should have an action plan to prevent state-sponsored murders.

A profoundly promising Black intellectual spoke on the impact of state sponsored murders committed against Black Americans. He proposed that White police abuse of authority should be considered a crime. Better known as Killer Mike, Michael Santiago Render also said that any police officer who kills outside of policy should be imprisoned for a period no less than twenty-five years. He further proposed that police who kill outside of policy should also have their pensions cut off and paid to the victim's family. Tax-payers should not be forced to pay for a crime they did not commit. In fact, he believes it's not the tax payers' responsibility to pay off law suits brought to the courts for adjudication.

Next, Killer Mike spoke about the premature training police undergo. He believes that police training should last longer than six to eight months. That police academies should be at least two years long, much like a junior college. The length of duration will ensure a better understanding of how to protect and serve American communities.

And lastly, Killer Mike, as he chooses not to identify by his government name, proposes that police candidates and cadets should also reflect or, at least, come from the communities they serve. If not, then he believes the government is creating a hunter and prey situation that can bring the country to the point of dispute needing intervention.

The second situation can be found in the public domain. Blacks do not trust nor accept rhetoric spoken by politicians. For generations, the only actions Blacks hear from politicians is empty rhetoric. The persuasive speeches of politicians like Joe Biden, Bill Clinton, both Bushes, and others, lack both sincerity or meaningful content. This situation is not only characteristic of the amount of apathy found in American politics, it is regarded as effective in distracting Blacks to the exclusion of important goals. It also enables Black people to accept their fate or allow their situation to happen without active response or resistance. Thus, the situation of Black people in America becomes fragmented or an overextended problem that could have reversed their situation.

The third situation is the problem of nihilism itself. We are dealing with generations of White people who reject the idea of racial integration. Many of them follow the belief that they are victims of society's woeful ills. One such problem is the idea that racial diversity equals genocide. They believe that racial diversity will lead to the genetic annihilation of the White race, eventually around the world. For them, life is meaningless. So, they reject the notion of religious and moral principles and are cynical with respect to racial integration.

These people will avoid nonwhites at any cost. They are the foot soldiers of American Republicanism. And like most Republican supporters, they have no political strategy except to keep America segregated. They also choose to function away from the scenes of American politics. Whites are averse to change thus commit to conservative values and ideas. Indeed, they are stark supporters of political conservatism.

Cultural nihilism reinforces the fragmentation of progressive movements in American society, movements that could better the situation for Blacks in America. Further, cultural nihilism keeps Black people vulnerable. In a society filled with intergroup conflict and hostility, the main priority of the people should be public discourse and democratic accountability.

The above content is reflective of a greater problem that exist in American society. Although this chapter is in no way exhaustive, it does provide insight into why contemporary Black expressions offend White people. The purpose of this chapter is also to give an historical sketch of the role Blacks played in the development of America's innovations, inventions, and technologies. In the last and final chapter, we will discuss recreation as a Contemporary form of Black Expression.

Chapter 8

Recreation as a Contemporary Black Expression

A Manner of Expression

…keep the political commentary to yourself or as someone once said,
"Shut up and dribble!"

Laura Ingraham (2018)

National Basketball League (NBA) All-Star legend LeBron James had a unique opportunity to speak about social injustice on National television. Unfortunately, Laura Ingraham publicly denounced LeBron, and then told him to shut up and dribble.

It is easy to understand why Blacks are motivated to succeed at sports, to be the best at what they do, even in terms of recreation. Unlike the arterial motives of their oppressors, the confidence they receive from succeeding gives them the feeling of achievement, and in making the world a better place, at least, in that moment.

I recognize that poverty is the motivation behind Black success. However, it involves much more than creating a need or not meeting basic needs. *Poverty* involves not having the simple means to effectively deal with changes in the environment. Blacks frustrate, not only because poverty does not satisfy their basic physiological needs, but since people have an internal need to effectively interact with their environment.

We are tactile creatures by nature. It's only natural for humans to seek out interaction rather than to reduce the urge or need to interact. Under present conditions, Blacks cannot effectively interact with their environment.

Aggression is an emotional outlet. It is one way to cope and reduce the cultural impact of stress and oppression.

There are various dimensions of culture. Many of these dimensions influence stress and coping. The one we are particularly interested in today and in this chapter is poverty.

Poverty imposes considerable stress on people. Poor people confront potent stressors everyday. Inadequate housing, dangerous neighbor-hoods, burdensome respons-ibilities, and economic uncertainties are among the many stressors poor people confront in their daily lives. An identity group particularly stressed out by the effects of poverty is Blacks.

Blacks endure chronic living conditions due to poverty. Many endure threatening and uncontrollable life events. For example, Blacks are more likely to experience crime and violence than a middleclass male who lives in an affluent White community. Blacks also live in conditions that undermine the sources of social support needed to help them buffer the effects of stress. What that means for Blacks is having to endure overburdened and unresponsive bureaucratic systems, many of which have them surviving below the minimum level of subsistence, which no person should have to exist. In this case, chronic living conditions contribute to their sense of powerlessness. The lack of available resources increases the likelihood they will experience crime and violence throughout their lifetime. However, there are social resources available to impoverished Blacks.

Recreation and Contemporary
Black Expressions

Recreation is a social resource done for enjoyment often when a person is not working or is vacationing from work and has the time to pursue leisurely interests. There are many forms of recreation. Each one can help reduce the social impact of stress and poverty.

Roller-skating is one of many recreational activities Blacks use as a social resource support to relieve the impact of poverty. Originally a recreational activity for children, roller-skating quickly became a leisure activity for Black adults in the 1960's and 1970's. Today, roller-skating rinks are spaces where adults come together to socialize.

At the height of the grove era (late 1970's), indoor roller-skating became a cultural fad. Young Blacks from innercities, who began skating early in life, skated well into adulthood, establishing a national trend. Called Black skate culture, many adult Blacks gathered, socially, for skate night at roller-skating rinks around the country. They roller-skated and danced around skating rinks to recorded music, most of which was disco music from the grove era.

In the 1960's, during segregation, Blacks were socially excluded from participating in roller-skating at skate clubs and skating parties across America. But, that did not stop them from partaking in that American pastime. In fact, Black skaters fought in protest to secure their place among White skaters in roller-skating rinks around America. In many cases, in social spaces where Blacks won approval, they were given the right to skate but only during Black-only skate nights. Mandated segregation in roller-skating rinks is how the term Black skate culture came into existence.

Today, roller-skating is a national treasure and an American pastime for Black people. It's one of a few leisure activities Blacks can enjoy away from the daily hassles of poverty. Although there are Whites who still show resistance, most of them do not understand the love affair Black people have with roller-skating.

Roller-skating allows Blacks to express themselves freely and openly. Sometimes, Blacks are under continuous stress, even while at the roller-skating rink. But, once they get into the spirit of roller-skating, they are able to get past their anxieties and become totally absorbed in the moment. The feeling of joy that comes from skating gives them that moment of freedom. It's the freedom of expression they cling to or that spills over into their daily lives.

Freedom of expression can cause social problems between Whites and Blacks. Roller-skating gives Blacks the freedom to express themselves in symbolic ways. That doesn't always translate well in the real world. Sometimes it just causes greater resistance from Whites, another cultural discrepancy existing between two separate and distinct cultural systems. Most times, that ability to openly express one's self is more than enough to help the individual learn to control their emotions.

The grove era of roller disco made its debut in the 1970's. It also helped to usher in a new era of the Black skate culture. In addition, it helped to create one of the most impactful revolution the world ever witnessed: the Hip-Hop revolution.

Hip-Hop as a Recreation and Contemporary Black Expression

Music has always been a wonderful form of recreation. And if you have a bit of rhythm, you can enjoy dancing to the groove or to the beat of music. From classical ballroom dancing to tap dancing, it can truly be inspirational. But, for me, there is nothing more awe inspiring than dancing to the wonderful beats of the streets.

No one actually knows where it originated. But, New York is the best known origins for this genre. Hip-Hop officially began on the mean streets of the Bronx, New York (early 1970's). It was a collaboration of intersecting groups like Blacks, Latinx, and Caribbean American youth who participated in community social gathering at Block parties. The music featured disc jockeys (DJ's) who began to isolate the percussion breaks of funk, soul, and disco songs and then extending it.

Rapping, which is a large part of Hip-Hop music, started when Masters of Ceremonies (MC's) were tasked with introducing DJ's and igniting the audience. They would talk, rhythmically, in between songs, kidding around and interacting with people in the audience. What started out as a recreational activity on the streets of New York, quickly became a local trend. The media called it a craze or fad. But, Hip-Hop quickly became a culture for Blacks, Latinx, and Caribbean youth, a few Whites too.

It appears that Hip-Hop satisfied the basic physiological needs of nonwhites, many of whom were poor Black and Latinx. Hip-Hop not only allowed nonwhites to deal effectively with their environment, it allowed them to be adept at what they were doing: inspiring happiness among the poor. The scheme of Hip-Hop moved efficiently as most nonwhites believed they were making the world a better place.

Whether it's a recreation, movement, or revolution, many Whites are offended by Hip-Hop. To this day, mainstream culture fails to understand what the hype is all about. But, humans have an internal drive to effectively interact with their environment. Hip-Hop is a way for them to do just that. And, they feel damn good about it. They are changing the scheme of culture, making America more assessable.

Curiously, by late 1970's and early 1980's, Teena Marie and the music band Blondie would compete for the first White recording artist to rhyme a song in rhythm. Although we know rap music started in a borough of the Bronx, it was introduced into the cultural mainstream by the music band Blondie. I told you there were a few Whites involved in the Hip-Hop revolution.

Is Rapture by Blondie the first rap song? No, but it is officially considered the first rap video ever broadcast on MTV; and that's an amazing feat! Rapture, sung by singer Debby Harry, also featuring Fab Five Freddy, one of the founding fathers of rap music, was released in 1980. Around the same time, it was Teena Marie, a White woman, on stage rapping to a West Coast beat. Although, her inspirational rap song, Square Biz, may have had more to do with Rick James and his influence on her music career, Teena Marie awakened the West coast with her vibrant sound.

No one seems to understand how or why a recreational activity like Hip-Hop would have the ability to motivate a crowd or inspire entire music genres, movements, and causes, social and political. There's even a revolution in place. It has taken off globally and is changing the thinking strategies of homogeneous societies worldwide.

The Hip-Hop revolution is single-handedly changing the social order of life. Not only is Hip-Hop taking over societies, it is teaching our young how to express themselves against existing powers of authority. And, Whites are offended by it. Why? Well first, it communicates significant points of political, social, and moral importance to the powers that be. It also communicates highly political messages about the social injustices and inhumane treatment of Blacks in America. Finally, many people feel that the culture is brash.

However, Hip-Hop took a substantial hit by the White establishment in Washington, DC. The government tempted to reign control over the movement as many politicians believed that rap music was poisoning the minds of mainstream children in America. Déjà vu? Government officials attempted to stop a movement similar to Rock and Roll in the 1950's. Rappers or free-style recording artists and break-dancers (recreational street dancers connected to Hip-Hop) suffered the ill-effects of police abuse and official murders across America from the police. The problem was not in the music itself, but the messages it delivered across racial boundaries.

Afrika Bambaataa is one of the originators of the breakbeat. He also gets credit for developing Hip-Hop culture. He had the ability to unify existing groups of people who fought against one another. This, he did by teaching them how to breakdance. So, when he began to unite street gangs and influenced others to call for a truce, the government feared losing control of its country. But with the loss of so many street artists, and the chronic living conditions of poor nonwhites, the time was right for them to alert the world of a war waged largely against our most vulnerable.

In the controversial rap song, Fuck The Police, hardcore rap group Niggers With Attitudes started a controversy that heightened tensions between two racially distinct groups, and forever changed the sociopolitical landscape of culture. The message delivered in the rap song warned the world about the realities of racism in America. And with entire cultures pleading for positive change, America was forced to reconsider its racial policies against Blacks, Latinx, and others.

Today, dominant society continues to be resistant to the idea of Hip-Hop. Its music, culture and movement are considered too brash or abrasive for consumer consumption. However, it continues to impact the lives of countless people. Once, White children listened to genres such as opera and classical music. Today, it's the rapper Future who's trending. Rock n' Roll is no longer at the center of mainstream culture, either. It is a dying art, with rock bands like Anvil losing out to this cultural juggernaut we call Hip-Hop. Even popular music is losing traction in the cultural mainstream. Hip-Hop culture has over-whelmed the cultural mainstream. Even the Super Bowl is being invaded with rappers like 50 Cent, Eminem, Dr. Dre, and Snoop Dogg who took the stage by storm during halftime.

Sports as a Contemporary Black Expression

Does anyone remember Super Bowl XLVII? The Ravens defeated the 49ers by a score of 34–31. It was the first time in the National Football League (NFL) that the San Francisco 49ers loss a Super Bowl in their franchise history. And what about the big upset during the game when the Ravens were winning by a substantial margin, you know, when the stadium experienced a power failure for approximately 30 minutes? What an impactful moment in NFL history. Oh, the emotions, the anxieties, that's the reason why I never watch sports; it's too emotional for me.

I can remember, back in the day, loving sports, playing the game, any game. Heck, I still do love playing sports. I just don't like watching it, on television or in person. I've also learned to be very competitive over the years. The psychology of the game, the motivation behind it, sports was an integral part of my upbringing. Hell, it's not just sports; it's part of the American dream.

To be an athlete in America is, perhaps, one of the most exciting careers a person can have. Ever since Jackie Robinson broke the racial barrier in major league baseball, sports have been a large part of the upbringing in Black households. Be it baseball, football, or track and field, playing sports as a career has been a dream of many, perhaps, a dream deferred for most.

Sports is one of the most accessible careers to Black people. In fact, it is one of the only careers readily accessible to Blacks. So, they choose to play sports and play it well. From the age of three to four-years, Black parents try to increase their children's motivations for playing sports. If you ever wondered why Blacks are so good at it, that's the reason. Believe it or not, Black people envision sports as a way out of their living situation. So, special emphasis is given to playing.

Now, the cultural stereotype is that Blacks were bread for physical activity thus are better adapted to play sports. This follows the belief that Blacks are brutish, lazy, morally degenerate, and dangerous. The majority of Whites are aligned with that line of argument. And they perpetuate it even though the belief is unfounded. Even the laws in place today perpetuate the interests of Whites based on cultural stereotypes created about Blacks. The result is many White people believe in the misconception about Blacks. Therefore, they find Blacks to be very offensive.

I guess to answer a few questions, you would have to understand how long it takes to breed athletic children. You would also have to answer the question of would it happen faster if you first bread out the intelligence in children. If those questions sound like it's bordering on eugenics, that's because it is. This is why some Black parents place special emphasis on increasing their children's intelligence and motivation for learning instead of playing sports.

The problem occurs when Black families follow the sports path. Many of them are so busy building a sports career for their children, they fail to place emphasis on education. Their first mistake occurs when they mole their children into the cultural image of a Black athlete. They are four times more likely to encourage their children to become athletes, even to the detriment of their intellectual and personal development.

Of the many Black high school sports enthusiasts, only five percent of them go on to play sports at the four-year college level. The greater majority become overwhelmed and frustrated. Nearly seventy percent of them drop out of college. Less than two percent of the sports enthusiasts who make the draft pick, actually play professional sports. Of the chosen few, sixty percent of them play professional sports for a period of three to four years before they're out of a career. And, without the credentials or skills to start a new career, most Black athletes find themselves financially destitute.

One of the latest arguments among Blacks is how beneficial is it really to play sports? What are the psychological and motivational characteristics that develop from it? And, are we rearing two types of people, one who is very physical and the other who is an intellectual? While most people are gung-ho about playing sports, conscious Blacks believe their needs to be a balance. They feel like Black people can have both by taking the time out to engage in both activities. The only catch is parents need to inform their children about the realities of seeking out a sports career and thus be more mindful to academic achievements. In essence, there are benefits to having both.

For Black families that choose only to focus their children on sports, there are consequences. Many of their children lack in character, are brash and, as a consequence, have trouble controlling their emotions. Males, in general, express themselves in an outward manner. From an early age, male children develop their coping skills by engaging in recreational activities. Large interaction with children their age teaches them how to problem solve. Outdoor activities such as playing in the sandbox, tree climbing, and what we used to call rough-housing or wrestling leads to the development of decision-making, problem-solving and, eventually, coping skills. The results are males learn in early childhood how to control their emotions. Sports is one of the main ways young males learn to control their emotions, assuming there is a balance.

Women, on the other hand, are at the opposite end of the gender continuum. Many of them learn to read and write as a resource for controlling their emotions. The result is they become critical thinkers. But, historically, they fall short in the area of business and politics. Professional skills develop as a result of social interaction. In early childhood, males forge personal bonds with peers that build self-confidence and, ultimately, teaches them to control their emotions.

At one point in time, we believed women were born emotional. That it was part of their natural makeup. But that theory was too readily accepted. Today, we know women experience negativity from hearing words such as no, don't, and stop more than the average male. Stop trying to compete with men, don't set with your legs open and, no, it is unladylike are terms that create a situation where women become socially deprived, Black women more so than most. Although, social depravity has long-terms effects on people regardless of their sexual or gender identity.

Today, we see the impact of having a balance. What I mean to say is women who are raised having to set reasonable and personally meaningful goals do better in life than people who spend their waking moment educating themselves or just playing sports. They are flooding the professional world as congresswomen, astronauts, aerospace engineers, et cetera. Obviously, women who achieve a healthy balance learn to control their emotions.

The same rule applies to Blacks. Those who are raised having a balance of both education and sports learn to control their emotions better. Those who do not, typically burn out. In general, Blacks are taught to control their emotions. On the other hand, with no emotional support or resources to prevent burnout, they become depressed while others resort to poor behavior. The road to criminality is a long, arduous process. It is a slippery slope to contrary or forbidden behavior.

What We Can Do About It

What we can do to bring a better understanding to a bad situation is build stronger relationships. While it's true, at least, to some degree that Blacks come across to Whites as brash, understand it is due to their environmental dwellings. Blacks live in deprived areas of major cities and towns. Their residents did not happen by accident but by design. The government, under various administrations, worked to socially exclude and persecute Black people under the litigation of law. The destruction of the Black community is one of the major outcomes. So, what is needed to better intergroup relations cannot be achieved without first reestablishing the Black community.

To build stronger or better relationships, there needs to be a community of interest present. That cannot happen without the presence of three basic elements: there must be a code of conduct present, an independent economic system existing, and politicians, who work for the people, in office. The latter cannot happen unless they come from the community; and, there are too few, if any, Black communities in America.

To begin the process, we must preserve the integrity of Black folk. This can be done simply by rebuilding the Black community. Local organizers and community builders have to guide the people if Blacks are to reestablish some level of independence.

Step one in the process is the revitalization and planning of Black neighborhoods. Physically, Black neighborhoods must be imbued with new life and vitality. Revitalizing and planning begin at the grassroots level. The reason why is because Black neighborhoods are, basically, the blueprint to nation building. And with a thriving Black economy, there would be secular changes in contemporary Black expressions.

Step two is the actual rebuilding of Black communities. Black neighborhoods are what's left of once thriving Black communities. Once neighborhoods are restored and Black people have the moral courage or confidence to commit, they must rebuild communities, one community at a time. Today, most Black neighborhoods are rundown shantytowns consisting of large numbers of crude dwellings. But, the revitalization process will not happen unless there is a code of conduct set in place.

A code of conduct is a set of unwritten rules outlining the duties, responsibilities, and obligations of a nation, society, or community member. It also includes proper or ethical practices for a political party, an organization, or individual. This way of living includes ethical, honor and moral codes, as well as respecting religious laws and belief systems. In this way, Black communities can hold local politicians accountable. Once the people are in agreement and there is mutual respect among them, they will be working within a framework of the Black cultural tradition.

Step three in the process is to elect politicians who have the community's best interest at heart. These politicians need to be likeminded individuals who have the same interest and opinions as the neighborhood residents they represent. They must also share the objectives, goals, and concerns as community residents. It would also be helpful if these politicians had a personal stake in the community, you know, skin in the game or something other. That way, relationships are mutually beneficial.

What you may not have picked up on thus far is that the process or elements are interrelated parts thus interchangeable. In fact, you have to toggle between the concepts to succeed. Without the basic elements I mentioned just moments before, there can be no community. And without existing communities, there can be no true understanding between or among cultural systems. There can only be a truce.

That chapter was the last of eight. Perhaps, you will reflect on each one and say you learned something more about yourself and others around you. This book merely scratches the surface on understanding Blacks and why their contemporary expressions offend White people. But, it does provide important insight on how to cooperate with strangers and others. It is truly important for us to understand how to get along in our surrounding world. And, for most Americans, it should start with understanding the Black experience in America. One of the most important events in this book is the resolution sections found after each chapter. Following this chapter, you will find an Epilogue that gives a closer look at breakdancing as a contemporary Black expression.

A Manner of Expression

Epilogue
More on Breakdancing
as a Contemporary Black Expression

A Manner of Expression

Much of what Black culture is White people refuse to acknowledge. The fact that Black people westernized Whites speaks to the possibility that Whites have assumed Black people's rightful identity and vice versa. Break-dancing is an example of how a people can create a culture from the depths of poverty and oppression. It's the creative processes of the contemporary Black expression that you should carry beyond this book, creativity that will enable you to better understand a people who struggle to find their rightful identity and the reasons why.

Breakdancing is one of the most artistic forms of contemporary Black expressions. It is an energetic dance form created and popularized by Black and indigenous (Latinx) Americans. It includes stylized footwork and athletic dance moves rooted in martial arts and gymnastics.

Breakdancing is the original dance style of Hip-Hop culture. Its origins date back as early as the 1950's to 1960's, starting with Black tap dancers and stage enter-tainers like Bill Bailey. Bill Bailey, a Black entertainer, debuted the moonwalk at the Apollo Theatre in New York 1955. He and entertainers like Sammie Davis Junior captivated their audiences with dance routines that would serve as the blueprint for breakdancing in the next generation. Though not greatly recognized in the Black prophetic tradition, their performances revolutionized dancing and changed the homogeneous thinking strategies of White people globally.

Today, the fancy dance routines and ground-breaking dance moves of b-boys and b-girls symbolizes the rough and hostile lifestyles that exist in ghettos across America. The dance moves are performed in tandem to look as if two or more break-dancers are fighting it out over scores of surfs.

Somewhere lost amid all of this is Afrika Bambaataa. Afrika Bambaataa is not only known for originating the breakbeat and a series of electronic tracks that influenced the development of Hip-Hop culture, on the innercity streets across America, he is known for bringing dance moves from Nigeria in Africa and the United States together into one artform: breakdancing.

Bambaataa used breakdancing to help bring peace to New York street gangs riddled with violence. Back then, the dance craze singled-handedly stopped crime, seemingly across the nation. The sudden calm of innercity streets threatened the stability of the US government. Many of its members, in fearing that a coup was underway, were quick to persecute break-dancers and existing members of Hip-Hop culture.

Whites across America would condemn breakdancing. Many of them considered it to be an artistic attempt at freestyle dancing. Others called it an ignorant artform used by untalented street-performers who were looking to earn change from business professionals and bystanders, many of whom sympathized with the efforts of impoverished innercity youth. Ironically, tap dancing began the same way: on the streets in front of nightclubs in New York City.

Today, the greater majority of break-dancers are White with Asians making up the next largest demographic. The number of performers is increasing worldwide with breakdancing soon to make its global debut in the Olympics (2024).

Throughout much of its history, break-dancing has not had a fair deal. Its early days represent a unique opportunity for innercity youth to make important contributions to our understanding of culture and the human condition. We not only need to improve our understanding of what change brings, we also need to better understand how anyone can make important contributions to human society as a whole, contributions that, quite frankly, can change the sociopolitical landscape of culture forever.

This book is meant to aid you in your journey to improve your understanding of Blacks and why they stand out as unique in this White dominated society we call the United States of America. It will not only help you to improve your knowledge-base about Blacks and their struggles, it will give you important insight into creating a more sociable and enjoyable environment for yourself and others. It may also help you to define yourself and the vastly changing world surrounding you.

References

Aleem, Z. (2022). 'The Squad' Could be Growing. But Will it Matter? Website [Online] Available: https://www.msnbc.com/opinion/msnbc-opinion/progressive-democrats-squad-midterms-rcna63677

Anderson, C. (2001). PowerNomics: The National Plan to Empower Black America. Bethesda, Maryland: PowerNomics Corporation.

Bradley, M. (1978). The Iceman Inheritance: Prehistoric Sources of Western Man's Racism, Sexism and Aggression. Kayode Publications

Britannica (2023). Breakdancing. Website [Online] Available: https://www.britannica.com/art/break-dance

Britannica (2023). Ebonics. Website [Online] Available: https://www.britannica.com/topic/ Ebonics

Business Insider Mexico (2020). All 4 Democratic Congresswomen of 'The Squad' are Heading Back to Congress: and with Backup. Website [Online Article] Available: https://businessinsider.mx/all-4-democratic-congresswomen-of-the-squad-are-heading-back-to-congress-and-with-backup/

CGTN America (2023). Black History Month: The Meaning of Soul Food. Social Media [Online] Available: https://www.youtube.com/watch?v=CX1RCdk3DwU

Christianity (2023). Slave Songs Transcended Sorrow Through Their Rich Lyrics and Meaning. Website [Online] Available: https://www.christianity.com/church/church-history/timeline/1601-1700/slave-songs-transcend-sorrow-11630165.html

DiAngelo, R. (2018). White Fragility: Why It's So Hard for White People to Talk About Racism. Boston, Massachusetts: Beacon Press

Holmes, K. C. (2008). Black Inventors: Crafting Over 200 Years of Success. Brooklyn, New York: Global Black Inventor Research Project.

Library of Congress (2023). African American Spirituals. Website [Online Article] Available: https://www.loc.gov/item/ihas.200197495/

Marsh, J. Mendoza-Denton, R. and Smith, J. A. (2010). Are We Born Racist? New Insights from Neuroscience and Positive Psychology. Boston, Massachusetts: Beacon Press.

MasterClass (2023). Hip-Hop Music Guide: History of Hip-Hop and Notable Artists. Website [Online] Available: https://www.masterclass.com/articles/hip-hop-guide

Maurer, D. W. (2023). (2023). Slang. Website [Online Britannica] Available: https://www.britannica.com/topic/slang

McGuire, B. C. (2020). <u>The Great Divide: The Social and Cultural Context of Inequality</u>. Windsor Mill, Maryland: Far-Left Publications.

McGuire, B. C. (2021). <u>Refusing to Learn: Really, How Dumb Do You Think I Am</u>? Windsor Mill, Maryland: Far-Left Publications.

McGuire, B. C. (2021). <u>Racism: The Behavioral Context of Intergroup Conflict and Hostility</u>. Windsor Mill, Maryland: Far-Left Publications.

McGuire, B. C. (2022). <u>Against Black People: The European Will To Conquer</u>. Windsor Mill, Maryland: Far-Left Publications.

Negro Spirituals (2023). <u>Negro Spirituals</u>. Website [Online] Available: https://www.negrospirituals.com/

NMAAHC (2023). <u>Gestures of Solidarity in African American Culture</u>. Website [Online Article] Available: https://nmaahc.si.edu/explore/stories/gestures-solidarity-african-american-culture

Ogbar, J. O. G. (2007). <u>Hip-Hop Revolution: Cultural and Politics of Rap</u>. Lawrence, Kansas. University Press of Kansas.

Page, S. (2021). <u>Inside Nancy Pelosi's War with AOC and the Squad.</u> Website [Online Article] Available: https://www.politico.com/news/magazine/2021/04/15/nancy-pelosi-alexandria-ocasio-cortez-481704

PBS (2023). <u>Do You Speak American?</u> Website [Online Article] Available: https://www.pbs.org/speak/seatosea/americanvarieties/AAVE/ebonics/

Redbull (2023). <u>History of Breakdancing: A Breakdown of Important Events</u>. Website [Online Article] Available: https://www.redbull.com/ca-en/history-of-breakdancing

Rory, P. Q. (2019). <u>Hip Hop History: From the Streets to the Mainstream</u>. Website [Online] Available: https://iconcollective.edu/hip-hop-history/

Smithsonian Libraries (2023). <u>Slave Songs of the United States</u>. https://library.si.edu/digital-library/book/slavesongsofunit00alle

Sullivan, K. (2019). <u>Here Are the 4 Congress-women Known as 'The Squad' Targeted by Trump's Racist Tweets</u>. Website [Online Article] Available: https://www.cnn.com/2019/07/15/politics/who-are-the-squad/index.html

The Kennedy Center. (2023). <u>Hip Hop: A Culture of Vision and Voice</u>. Website [Online]. Available: https://www.kennedy-center.org/education/resources-for-educators/classroom-resources/media-and-interactives/media/hip-hop/hip-hop-a-culture-of-vision-and-voice/

Van Sertima, I. (1996). <u>They Came Before Columbus: The Presence in Ancient America</u>. New York: Random House.

Wikipedia (2023). <u>Hip Hop Music</u>. Website [Online] Available: https://en.wikipedia.org/wiki/Hip_hop_music

Wikipedia (2023). <u>Slave Songs of the United States</u>. Website [Online Article] Available: https://en.wikipedia.org/wiki/Slave_Songs_of_the_United_States

Wikipedia (2023). <u>The Squad (United States Congress)</u>. Website [Online Article] Available: https://en.wikipedia.org/wiki/The_Squad_(United_States_Congress)

Word Up Community Magazine (2023). <u>Food for the Soul: A Brief Look at the History of Soul Food in America</u>. Social Media [Online Documentary] Available: https://www.youtube.com/watch?v=bxSWSdhiWGY

Working Families Party (2022). <u>We're Standing with the Squad in 2022</u>. Website [Online Article] Available: https://workingfamilies.org/2022/03/were-standing-with-the-squad-in-2022/

A Manner of Expression

A Manner of Expression

www.ingramcontent.com/pod-product-compliance
Lightning Source LLC
Chambersburg PA
CBHW070656250726
48662CB00001B/144